Using the Standards
Geometry

Grade 2

Published by Instructional Fair
an imprint of
Frank Schaffer Publications®

Instructional Fair

Development House: MATHQueue, Inc.

Frank Schaffer Publications®

Instructional Fair is an imprint of Frank Schaffer Publications.

Printed in the United States of America. All rights reserved. Limited Reproduction Permission: Permission to duplicate these materials is limited to the person for whom they are purchased. Reproduction for an entire school or school district is unlawful and strictly prohibited. Frank Schaffer Publications is an imprint of School Specialty Publishing. Copyright © 2005 School Specialty Publishing.

Send all inquiries to:
Frank Schaffer Publications
3195 Wilson Drive NW
Grand Rapids, Michigan 49534

Using the Standards: Geometry—Grade 2

ISBN: 0-7424-2982-2

2 3 4 5 6 7 8 9 10 HIL 10 09 08 07

Table of Contents

Introduction................4–5
Standards Correlation Chart..6
Pretest....................7–8

Relationships
Lines and Line Segments......9
Lines that Cross Each Other...10
Rays and Angles.............11
Triangles...................12
Squares.....................13
Rectangles..................14
Circles.....................15
How Many?...................16
Sides of Polygons...........17
Parallel and Perpendicular
   Lines....................18
Quadrilaterals..............19
Parallelograms..............20
Trapezoids..................21
Pentagons...................22
Hexagons....................23
Octagons....................24
Regular and Irregular Figures.25
Finish the Drawing..........26
Joining Shapes..............27
Divide Into More............28
The Size of Shapes..........29
Types of Triangles..........30
Which Figure Am I?..........31
Solid Figures...............32
Objects that Model Solid
   Figures..................33
Face, Edges, and Vertices...34
Plane Figure or Solid Figure.35
Which Solid Figure Am I?....36
Stacking Solid Objects......37
Will It Roll?...............38
Create Your Own Problems....39
Check Your Skills.........40–41

Locations
The Toy Chest...............42
Three Letter Words..........43
Above and Below.............44
Going Shopping..............45
Sunny or Cloudy.............46
Study Time..................47
In the Fish Bowl............48
In Full Bloom............49–50
Directions to a Word........51
About the Town..............52
Polygon People..............53
End to End..................54
Length of Line Segments.....55
Plot for Distance...........56
Lines of Symmetry...........57
Picture of Symmetry.........58
Two Lines of Symmetry.......59
Draw with Symmetry..........60
More Pictures with Symmetry..61
Create Your Own Problems....62
Check Your Skills.........63–64

Transformations
Flips.......................65
Slides......................66
Turns in Both Directions....67
Show a Flip, Slide, and Turn..68
Transformations.............69
Match the Transformation....70
Transform Pattern Blocks..71–72
More Block
   Transformations........73–74
Split in Half?..............75
Symmetry in the World.......76
Many Lines of Symmetry......77
Point Symmetry..............78
Create Your Own Problems....79
Check Your Skills.........80–81

Modeling
Shapes in Your World........82
Solid Figures in Your World..83
Use Dot Paper to Draw.......84
More Dot Paper Drawings.....85
Match Maker.................86
Congruent Shapes............87
Perimeters on Dot Paper.....88
Areas on Dot Paper..........89
Draw a Cube Using
   Dot Paper................90
Rectangular Prism on
   Dot Paper................91
Draw Another Cube...........92
Draw Another Prism..........93
Draw a Cylinder.............94
Draw a Cone.................95
Draw a Sphere...............96
Net for a Cube..............97
Net for a Square Pyramid....98
Flat Surfaces and Corners...99
That's the Solid Figure....100
Rectangular Prism
   Dot-to Dot..............101
Square Pyramid Dot-to-Dot..102
Looking From a
   Different View..........103
Building Stacks............104
Act as a Builder...........105
Create Your Own Problems...106
Check Your Skills......107–108

Post Test..........109–110
Answer Key........111–120
Vocabulary Cards..121–128

Published by Instructional Fair. Copyright protected.

0-7424-2982-2 Using the Standards: Geometry

Introduction

This book is designed around the standards from the National Council of Teachers of Mathematics (NCTM), with a focus on geometry. Students will build new mathematical knowledge, solve problems in context, apply and adapt appropriate strategies, and reflect on processes.

The NCTM process standards are also incorporated throughout the activities. The correlation chart on page 6 identifies the pages on which each NCTM geometry substandard appears. Also look for the following process icons on each page.

 Problem Solving   Communication   Reasoning and Proof

 Connections   Representation

Workbook Pages: These activities can be done independently, in pairs, or in groups. The problems are designed to stimulate higher-level thinking skills and address a variety of learning styles.

Problems may be broken into parts, with class discussion following student work. At times solution methods or representations are suggested in the activities. Students may gravitate toward using these strategies, but they should also be encouraged to create and share their own strategies.

Many activities will lead into subjects that could be investigated or discussed further as a class. You may want to compare different solution methods or discuss how to select a valid solution method for a particular problem.

Communication: Most activities have a communication section. These questions may be used as journal prompts, writing activities, or discussion prompts. Each communication question is labeled **THINK** or **DO MORE**.

Introduction (cont.)

Create Your Own Problems: These pages prompt students to create problems like those they completed on the worksheet pages. Encourage students to be creative and to use their everyday experiences. The students' responses will help you to assess their practical knowledge of the topic.

Check Your Skills: These activities provide a representative sample of the types of problems developed throughout each section. These can be used as additional practice or as assessment tools.

Vocabulary Cards: Use the vocabulary cards to familiarize students with mathematical language. The pages may be copied, cut, and pasted onto index cards. Paste the front and back on the same index card to make flash cards, or paste each side on separate cards to use in matching games or activities.

Assessment: Assessment is an integral part of the learning process and can include observations, conversations, interviews, interactive journals, writing prompts, and independent quizzes or tests. Classroom discussions help students learn the difference between poor, good, and excellent responses. Scoring guides can help analyze students' responses. The following is a possible list of problem-solving steps. Modify this list as necessary to fit specific problems.

1—Student understands the problem and knows what he or she is being asked to find.

2—Student selects an appropriate strategy or process to solve the problem.

3—Student is able to model the problem with appropriate manipulatives, graphs, tables, pictures, or computations.

4—Student is able to clearly explain or demonstrate his or her thinking and reasoning.

NCTM Standards Correlation Chart

		Problem Solving	Reasoning and Proof	Communication	Connections	Representation
Relationships	recognize, draw, and compare 2-D and 3-D shapes	25, 28,	12, 16, 17, 18,	9, 10, 11,	33, 35,	10, 11, 13, 14, 15,
	describe attributes of 2-D and 3-D shapes	31, 37	19, 22, 23, 24,	13, 26, 27,	37, 38	16, 19, 20, 21, 22,
	put together and take apart 2-D and 3-D shapes		25, 26, 29, 31, 34, 36, 38	30, 32		23, 24, 27, 28, 30, 32, 33, 34, 35, 36
Locations	describe position describe direction and distance name locations	42, 49, 50, 51, 56, 60	45, 55, 58, 59	42, 43, 44, 47, 48, 51, 52, 53, 57, 58, 59, 60, 61	43, 45, 46, 47, 48, 52, 61	44, 46, 49, 50, 53, 54, 57
Transformations	recognize and apply flips, slides, and turns	68, 70	65, 66, 67, 75, 76, 77, 78	69, 70, 71, 72, 73, 74, 78	67, 76	65, 66, 67, 68, 69, 71, 72, 73, 74, 75, 77
	recognize and create shapes that have symmetry					
Modeling	use spatial visualization draw from different perspectives relate ideas to number and measurement recognize shapes	87, 88, 89, 103, 104	87, 99, 100	99, 105	82, 83, 105	82, 83, 84, 85, 86, 88, 89, 90, 91, 92, 93, 94, 95, 96, 97, 98, 100, 101, 102, 103, 104

The pretest, post test, Create Your Own Problems, and Check Your Skills pages are not included on this chart, but contain a representative sampling of the process standards. Many pages also contain THINK or DO MORE sections, which encourage students to communicate about what they have learned.

Published by Instructional Fair. Copyright protected.

0-7424-2982-2 Using the Standards: Geometry

Name _____ Date _____

Pretest

1. Draw a line segment. Label the endpoints A and B.

2. Circle the name of the shape below.

      parallelogram

   rhombus

   trapezoid

3. Which solid figure has 6 faces of equal size?

   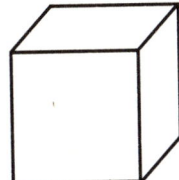   cube

   sphere

   triangle

4. Circle the object left of . Put an X over the object above .

Name _____ Date _____

Pretest (cont.)

5. Is the line shown on the rectangle a line of symmetry? Circle the correct answer.

   yes   no

6. Connect the points. Then name the shape drawn.

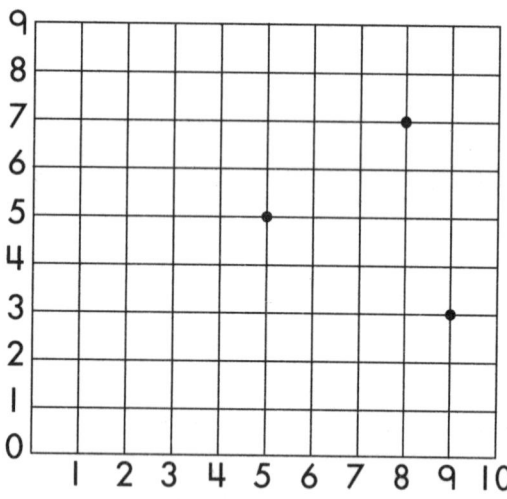

_____

7. Which transformation is shown? Circle the correct answer.

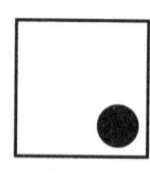 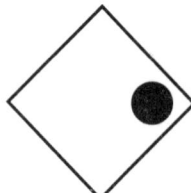

slide

flip

turn

8. Number the squares below so that 1 is the smallest square and 3 is the largest square.

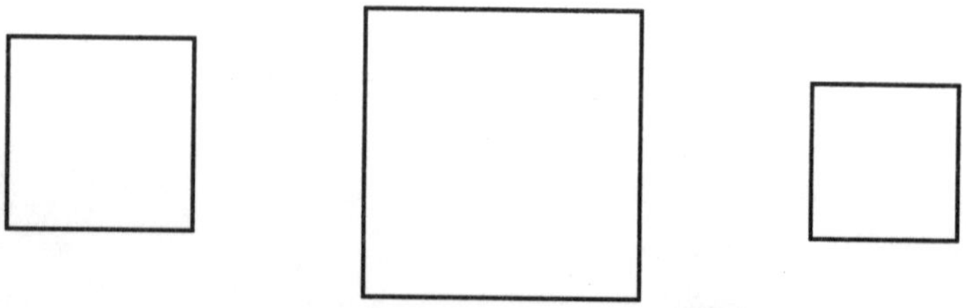

Published by Instructional Fair. Copyright protected.   0-7424-2982-2 Using the Standards: Geometry

Relationships

Name _____ Date _____

Lines and Line Segments

A **line** goes on in both directions forever.

A **line segment** has two endpoints.   S•———————•T

Directions: Trace the dashed line and arrows. Draw two more lines.

1. ←– – – – – – – – – – – →

2.

3.

Directions: Trace the dashed line segments. Connect the endpoints to draw two more line segments.

4. N •– – – – – – – – – – – • M

5. C•   D•

6. X•
        Y•

THINK

Which can you measure with a ruler, a line or a line segment?

Relationships     Name _____   Date _____

Lines that Cross Each Other

Lines that cross each other are **intersecting lines.**

Directions: Draw another line for each line so that the two lines intersect.

1.

2.

3.

4.

5.
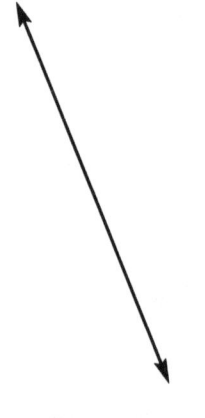

6.

Relationships     Name _____ Date _____

Rays and Angles

A **ray** has one endpoint and goes on in the other direction forever.

Two rays with a common endpoint form an **angle**.

An angle that forms a square corner is a **right angle**.

This symbol means right angle.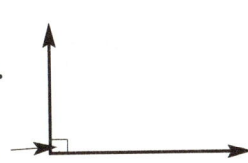

Directions: Circle the word that names each figure.

1.

   angle   ray

2.

   ray   right angle

3.

   ray   right angle

4.

   angle   ray

5.

   right angle   angle

6.

   angle   ray

THINK    Imagine 2 rays that share an endpoint, and go in opposite directions. What do the rays look like?

Relationships

Name _____ Date _____

Triangles

A **triangle** has 3 sides and 3 vertices.

side

vertex

Vertices is the plural of vertex.

Directions: Trace the dotted line segments to draw a triangle. Draw 3 more triangles.

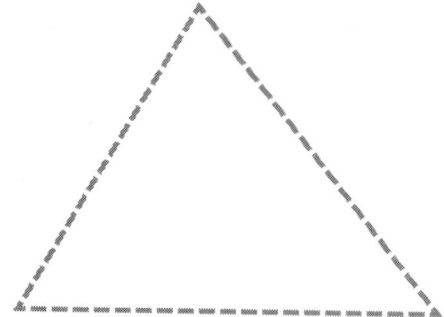

DO MORE

When one vertex is a right angle, the triangle is a right triangle. Draw a right triangle.

12

Published by Instructional Fair. Copyright protected.

0-7424-2982-2 Using the Standards: Geometry

Relationships

Name _____ Date _____

Squares

A **square** has 4 sides and 4 vertices.

All 4 sides are the same length.
A square has 4 right angles.

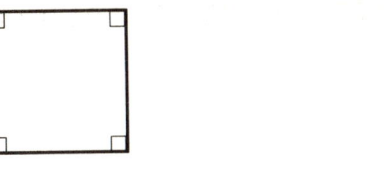

Directions: Trace the dotted line segments to draw a square. Draw 3 more squares.

Relationships  Name _____ Date _____

Rectangles

A **rectangle** has 4 sides and 4 vertices.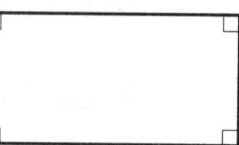

Opposite sides are the same length.
A rectangle has 4 right angles.

Directions: Trace the dotted line segments to draw a rectangle.
Draw 3 more rectangles.

DO MORE

 Draw a rectangle that is taller than it is long.

Relationships Name _____ Date _____

Circles

This is a **circle**.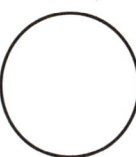

It has 0 sides.

Directions: Trace the dotted curve to draw a circle. Then find 2 round objects that you can trace around to draw 2 more circles.

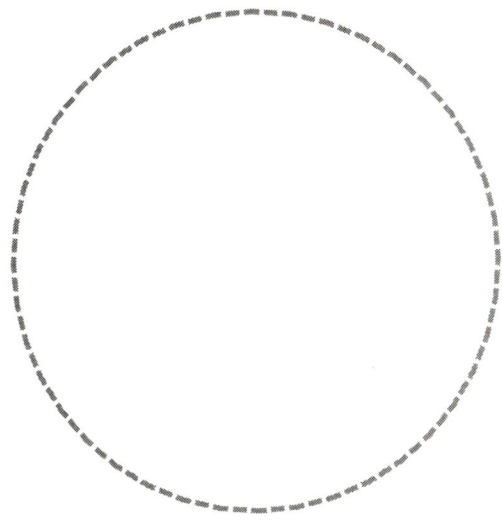

Relationships     Name _____   Date _____

How Many?

Directions: Write how many of each shape you see in each blank.

1. circle _____

2. rectangle _____

3. square _____

4. triangle _____

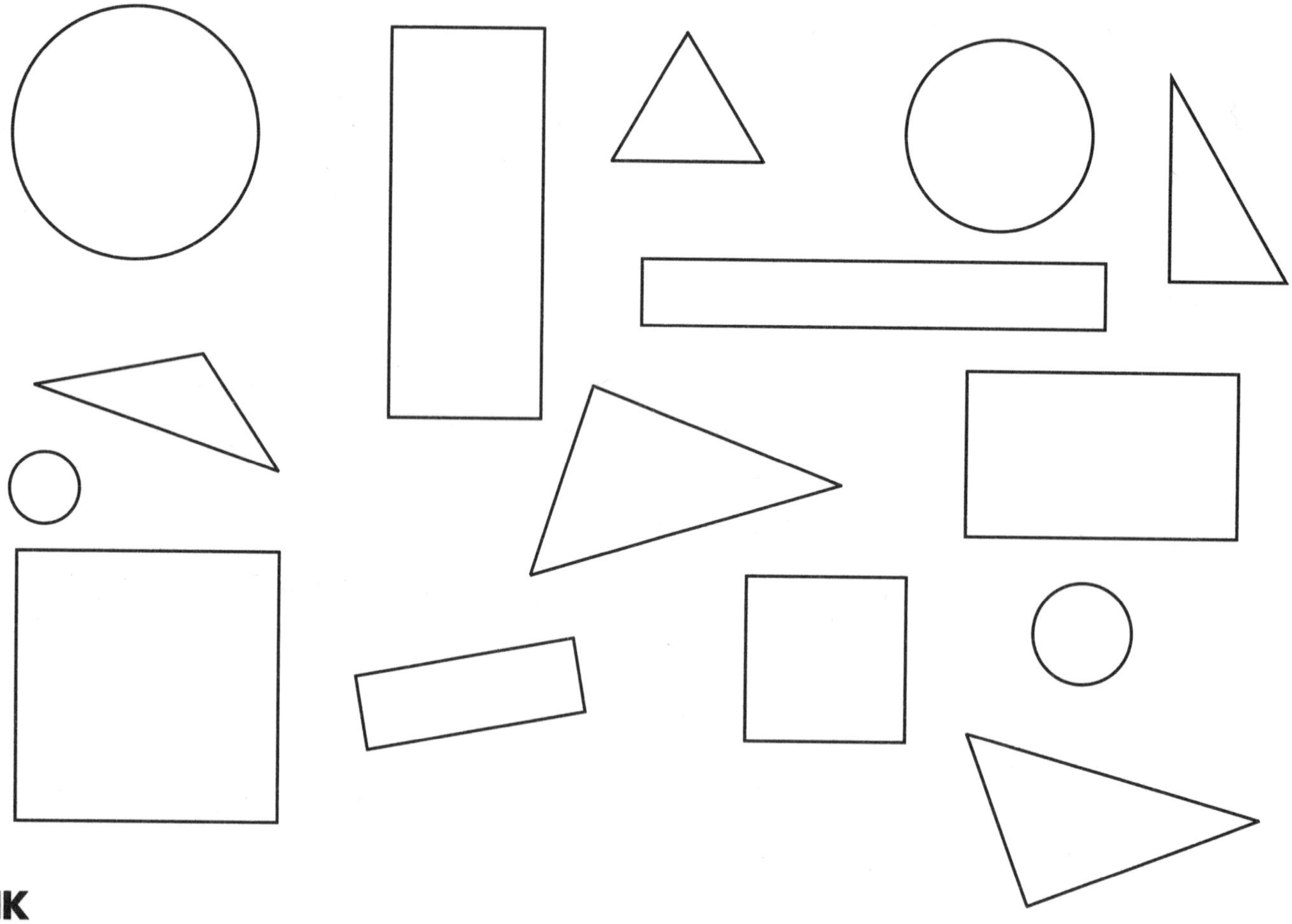

THINK

 A square is a special rectangle because all of its sides are the same length. Using this information how do your answers above change?

Relationships   Name _____ Date _____

Sides of Polygons

A **polygon** is a closed plane figure with 3 or more line segments.

Each **side** of a polygon is a line segment.
The point where two sides meet is a **vertex**.

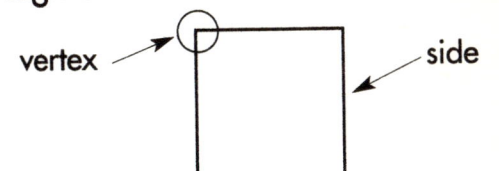

A **regular polygon** has sides and angles of equal measures.
An **irregular polygon** is a polygon that is not regular.

Directions: Count the number of sides and number of vertices for each polygon. Fill in the blanks.

1. 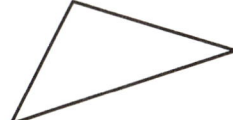   number of sides _____ number of vertices _____

2.    number of sides _____ number of vertices _____

3. 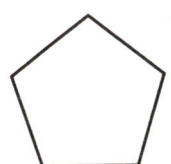   number of sides _____ number of vertices _____

4. 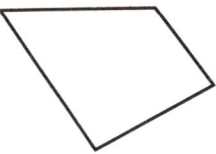   number of sides _____ number of vertices _____

THINK

 Is a circle a polygon? Why or why not?

 Relationships   Name _____   Date _____

Parallel and Perpendicular Lines

Lines that intersect each other to form right angles are **perpendicular lines**.

Lines that do not intersect each other are **parallel lines**.

Directions: Tell whether each set of lines is parallel, perpendicular, or neither. Circle the correct answer choice.

1.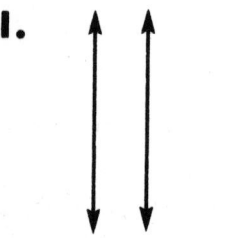

   parallel

   perpendicular

2.

   parallel

   perpendicular

3.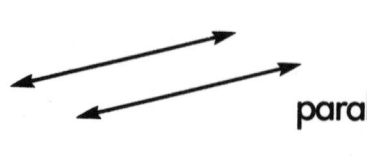

   parallel

   perpendicular

4.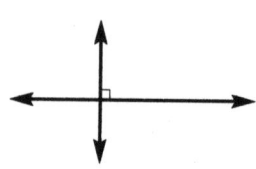

   parallel

   perpendicular

Directions: Draw a line that is parallel to each line. Draw another line that is perpendicular to each line.

5.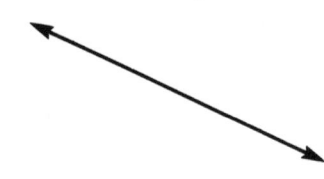

6.

Relationships

Name _____ Date _____

Quadrilaterals

A **quadrilateral** is a four-sided plane figure.
A **regular quadrilateral** has all four sides the same length.

regular quadrilaterals

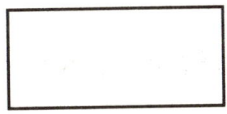
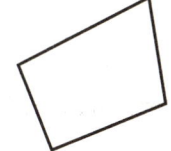

irregular quadrilaterals

Directions: Circle the answer choice that best names each figure.

1.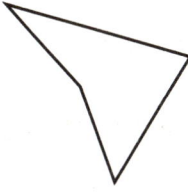
   regular quadrilateral
   irregular quadrilateral
   not a quadrilateral

2.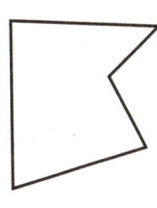
   regular quadrilateral
   irregular quadrilateral
   not a quadrilateral

3.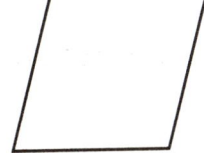
   regular quadrilateral
   irregular quadrilateral
   not a quadrilateral

4.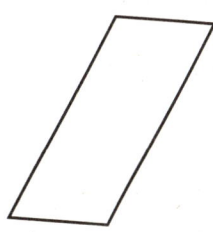
   regular quadrilateral
   irregular quadrilateral
   not a quadrilateral

THINK

Name a traffic sign that is a quadrilateral.

Relationships Name _____ Date _____

Parallelograms

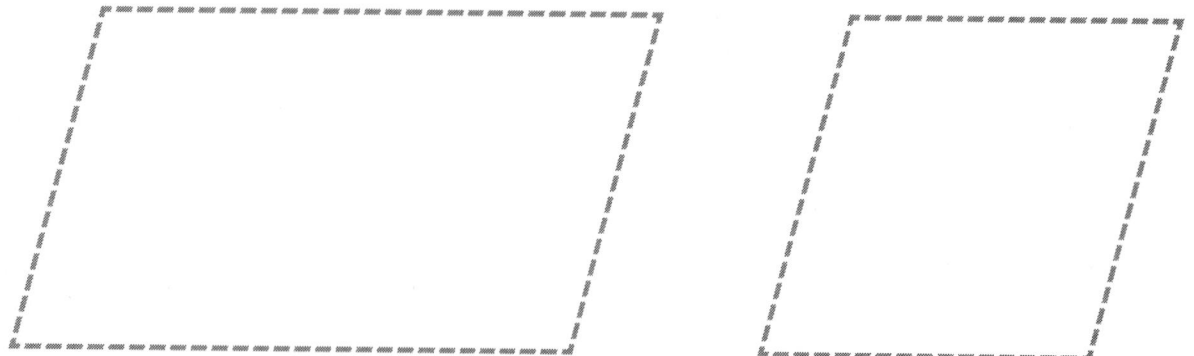

A **parallelogram** is quadrilateral with two pairs of parallel sides.
A **rhombus** is a parallelogram with all four sides the same length.

parallelogram   rhombus

Directions: Trace the dotted line segments to draw a parallelogram and a rhombus. Then draw one more parallelogram and one more rhombus.

Relationships   Name _____ Date _____

Trapezoids

A **trapezoid** is a quadrilateral with only one pair of parallel sides.
An **isosceles trapezoid** has two sides (not the parallel sides) the same length.

trapezoid   isosceles trapezoid

Directions: Trace the dotted line segments to draw a trapezoid. Then draw one more trapezoid and one isosceles trapezoid.

DO MORE

Use a crayon or marker to trace over the parallel sides in each trapezoid.

21

Published by Instructional Fair. Copyright protected.   0-7424-2982-2 *Using the Standards: Geometry*

| Relationships | Name _____ Date _____ |

Pentagons

A **pentagon** is a five-sided plane figure.
A **regular pentagon** has all five sides the same length.

regular pentagon 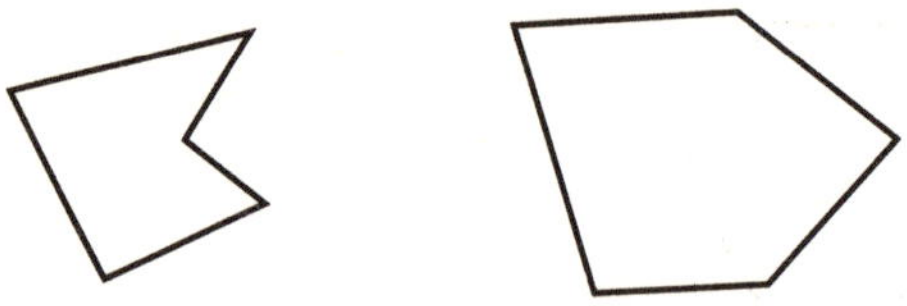   irregular pentagons

Directions: Circle the answer choice that best names each figure.

1. 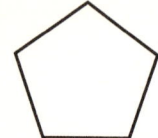   regular pentagon

   irregular pentagon

2.    regular pentagon

   irregular pentagon

Directions: Complete each drawing so that the figure is a pentagon.

3.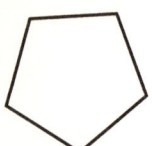

4.

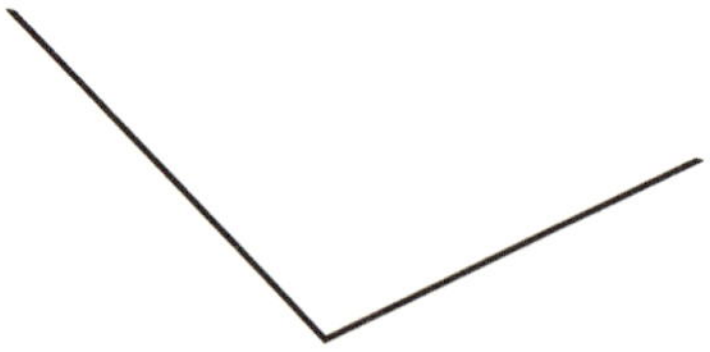

22

Published by Instructional Fair. Copyright protected.   0-7424-2982-2 *Using the Standards: Geometry*

Relationships

Name _____ Date _____

Hexagons

A **hexagon** is a six-sided plane figure.
A **regular hexagon** has all six sides the same length.

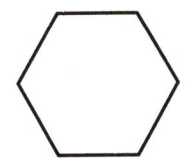
regular hexagon

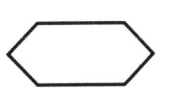
irregular hexagons

Directions: Trace the dotted line segments to draw a regular hexagon and an irregular hexagon. Draw one more irregular hexagon.

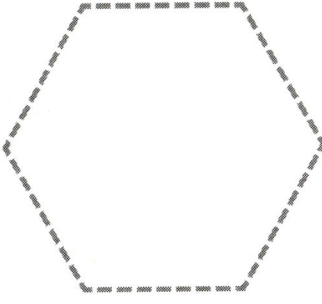   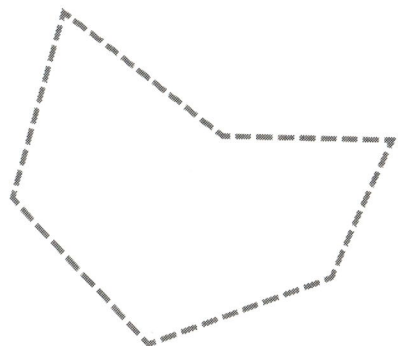

23

Published by Instructional Fair. Copyright protected.

0-7424-2982-2 *Using the Standards: Geometry*

Relationships

Name _____ Date _____

Octagons

An **octagon** is an eight-sided plane figure.
A **regular octagon** has all eight sides the same length.

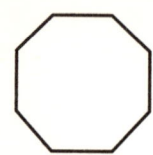
regular octagon

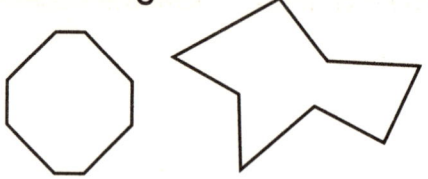
irregular octagons

Directions: Trace the dotted line segments to draw a regular octagon. Draw another octagon that is irregular.

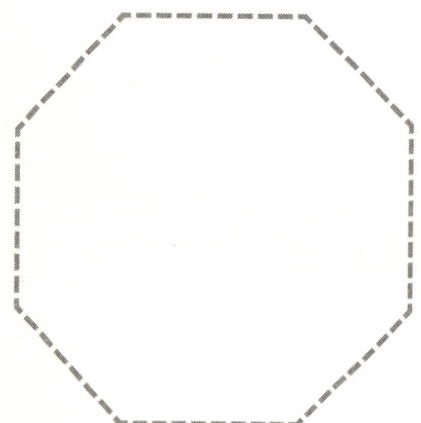

DO MORE

 Color and design the octagon above so that it looks like an object that you probably see everyday.

Relationships Name _____ Date _____

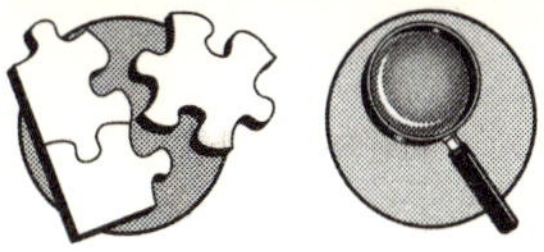

Regular and Irregular Figures

Directions: Match the name of each polygon to a regular polygon in the left column and an irregular polygon in the right column. Draw a line to show the matches.

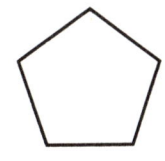   

                                    hexagon

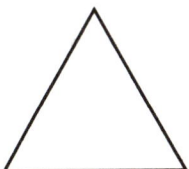   

                                    octagon

                                    pentagon

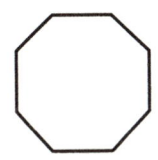   

                                    quadrilateral

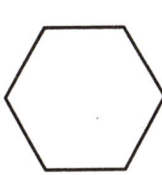   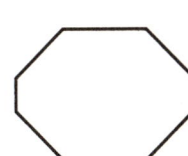

                                    triangle

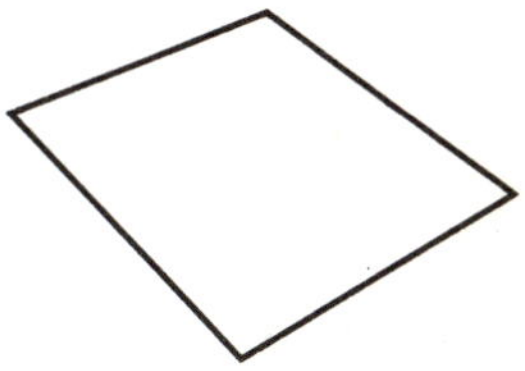

                                                                                      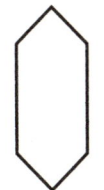

25

Relationships   Name _____   Date _____

Finish the Drawing

Directions: Use the line segments given to complete a drawing of each figure named.

1. pentagon

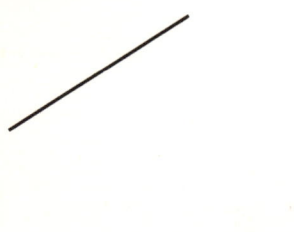

2. quadrilateral

3. hexagon

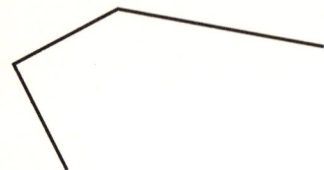

4. triangle

_____

THINK

In questions 2 and 4 above, which one would let you draw a regular polygon (all sides the same length) from the line segments given?

Relationships

Name _____ Date _____

Joining Shapes

Directions: Draw a new shape using the figures named for each.

 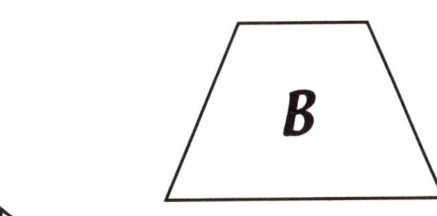 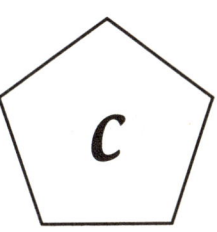

 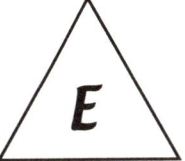

1. shapes *B* and *E*

2. shapes *A* and *D*

3. shapes *A* and *C*

4. shapes *B* and 2 of *E*

Relationships     Name _____   Date _____

Divide Into More

Directions: Draw line segments to divide each figure into the shapes named.

1. 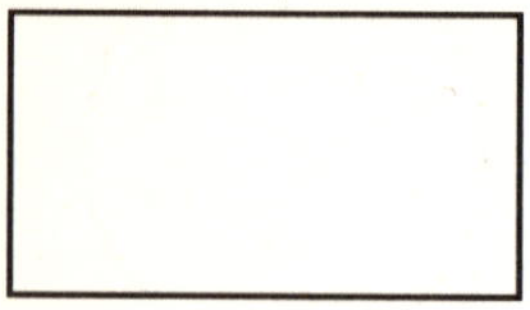 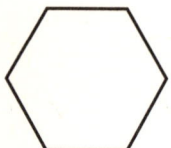   make 4 rectangles

2. 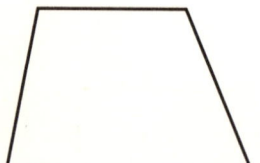   make 2 trapezoids

3. 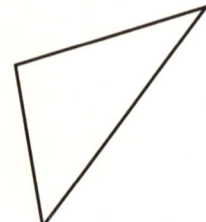   make 2 triangles

4.   make 2 triangles

DO MORE

 Draw a square. Draw two line segments to divide it into 4 triangles.

Relationships  Name _____ Date _____

The Size of Shapes

Directions: For each row of shapes, put an X over the smallest figure. Color the largest figure.

1.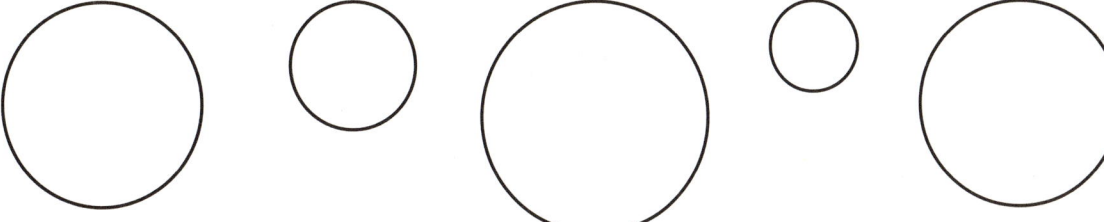

2.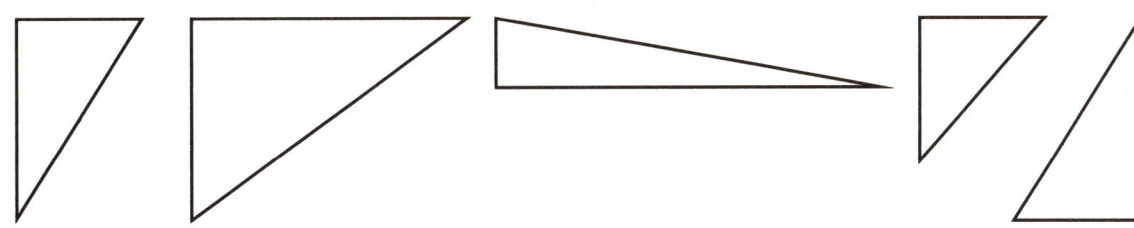

3.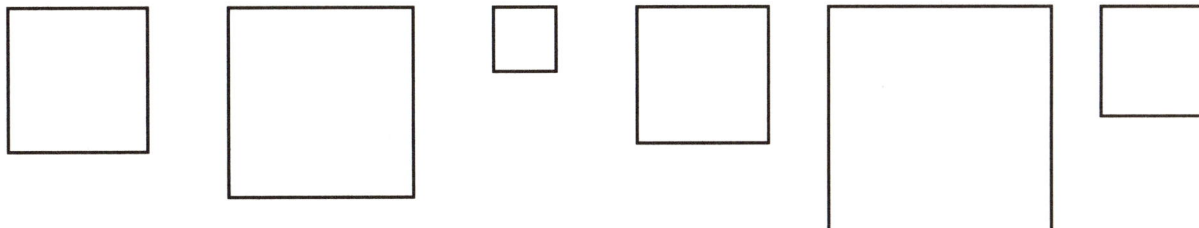

4.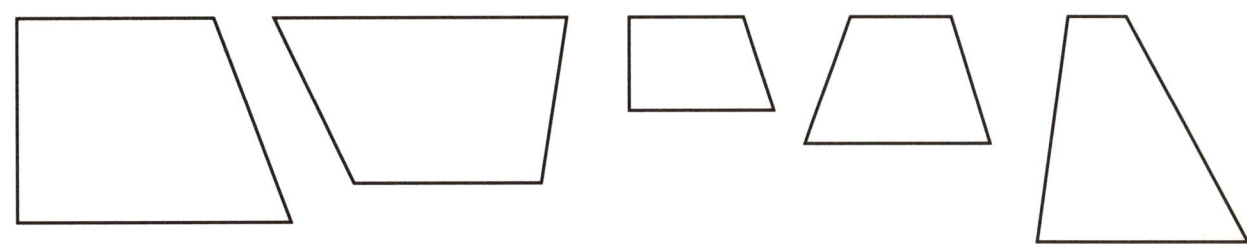

Relationships

Name _____ Date _____

Types of Triangles

An **equilateral triangle** has 3 sides of equal length.

An **isosceles triangle** has 2 sides of equal length.

A **scalene triangle** has no sides of equal length.

Directions: Name each triangle. Circle the correct answer.

1. 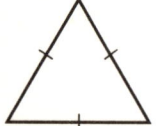   equilateral
   isosceles
   scalene

2. 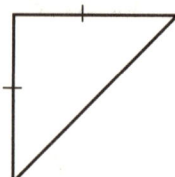   equilateral
   isosceles
   scalene

3. 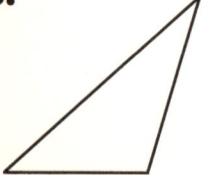   equilateral
   isosceles
   scalene

4.    equilateral
   isosceles
   scalene

THINK

Can an isosceles triangle also be an equilateral triangle?
Can a scalene triangle also be an isosceles triangle?

Published by Instructional Fair. Copyright protected.   0-7424-2982-2 *Using the Standards: Geometry*

Relationships

Name _____ Date _____

Which Figure Am I?

Directions: Circle each figure that is described.

1. I do not have any pairs of parallel sides.

   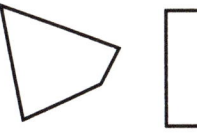  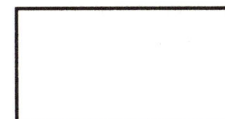 

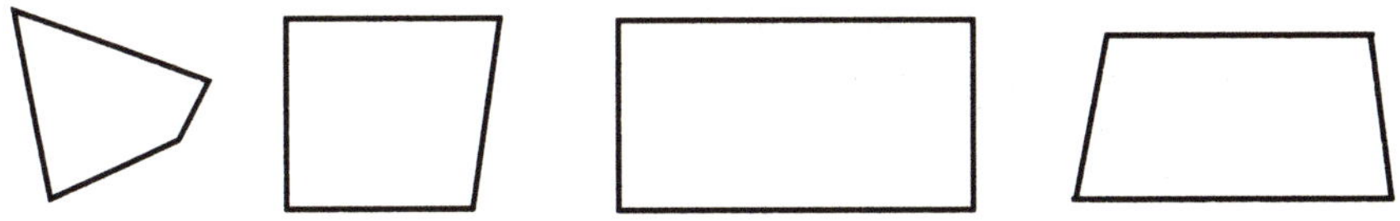

2. I have only one right angle.

   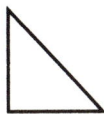   

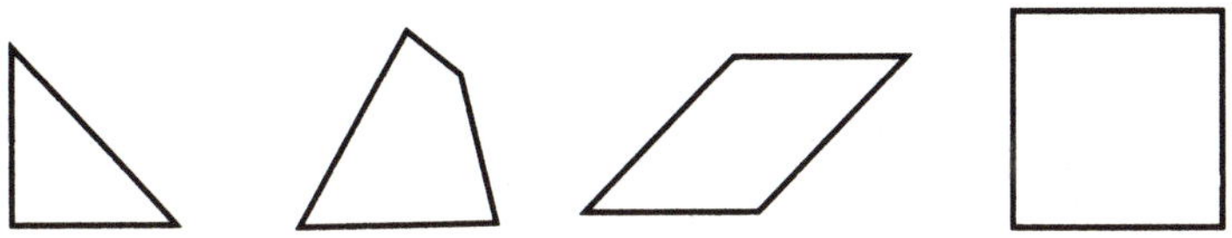

3. I have 4 right angles.

    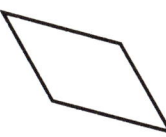 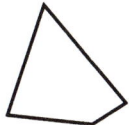 

4. I do not have 2 pairs of parallel sides.

    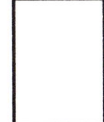  

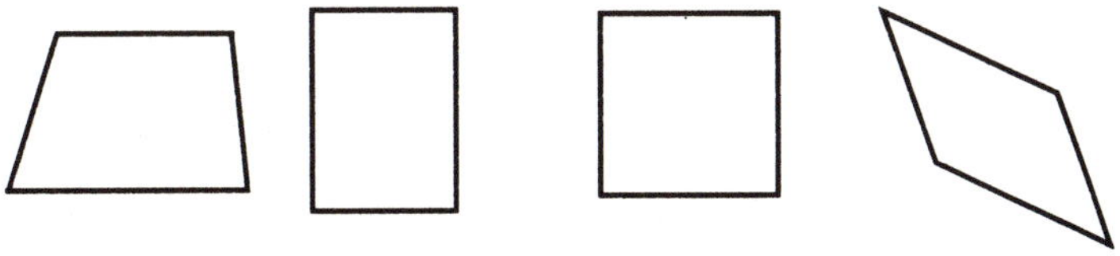

5. I have 2 pairs of parallel sides and no right angles.

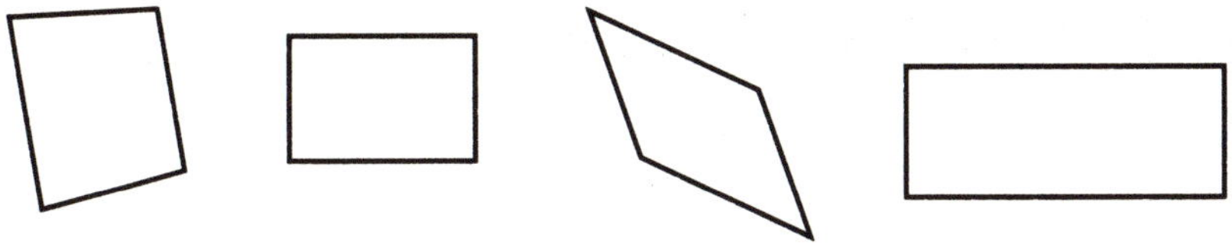

    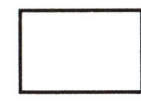 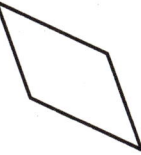 

DO MORE

Write a problem like the ones above to share with a friend.

Relationships Name _____ Date _____

Solid Figures

A **solid figure** is a 3-dimensional shape.

| cube | rectangular prism | cone | cylinder | sphere |

Directions: Write the name of each solid figure.

1. _____

2. 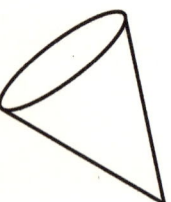 _____

3. _____

4. 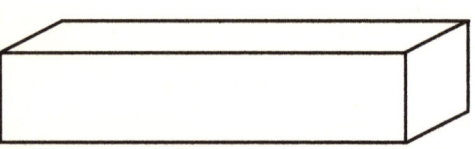 _____

Name _____ Date _____

Objects that Model Solid Figures

Directions: Name the solid figure that each object or objects model.

1.

_____

2.

_____

3.

_____

4.

_____

5.

_____

6.

_____

Relationships     Name _____   Date _____

Faces, Edges, and Vertices

A **face** is a flat surface of a solid figure.
The place where two faces of a solid figure meet is an **edge**.
The point where two or more edges meet is a **vertex**.

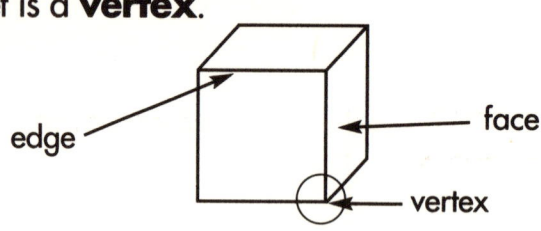

Directions: Fill in each blank.

1.

   number of faces _____   number of edges _____

2.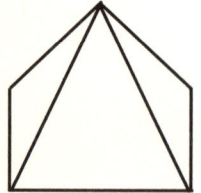

   number of edges _____   number of vertices _____

3.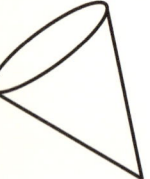

   number of faces _____   number of vertices _____

4.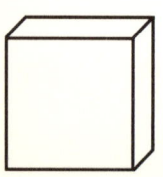

   number of edges _____   number of vertices _____

Relationships   Name _____ Date _____

Plane Figure or Solid Figure

Directions: Identify each object as a plane figure or a solid figure. Circle the correct answer choice.

1. 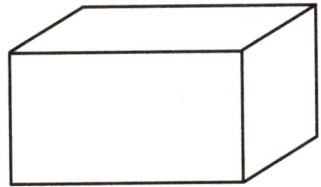   plane figure   solid figure

2. 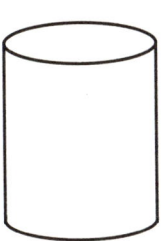   plane figure   solid figure

3. 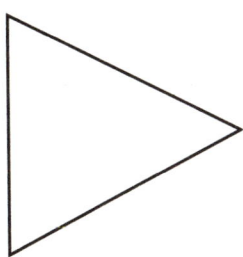   plane figure   solid figure

4. 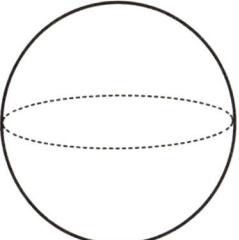   plane figure   solid figure

Name _____ Date _____

Which Solid Figure Am I?

Directions: Which solid figure is described? Circle each figure.

1. I am made of 6 squares.

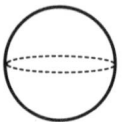 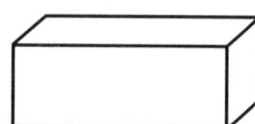 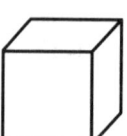 

2. I have two circular bases.

 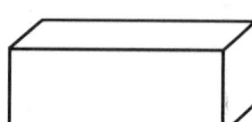 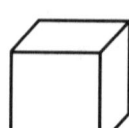 

3. I have one circular base and a vertex.

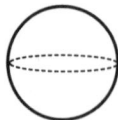 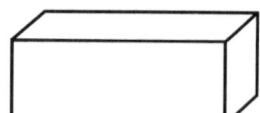 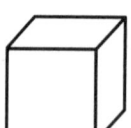 

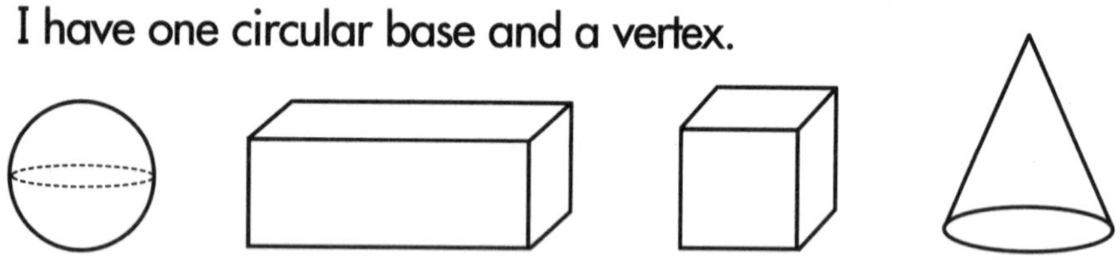

4. All of my faces are rectangles.

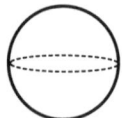 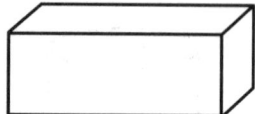  

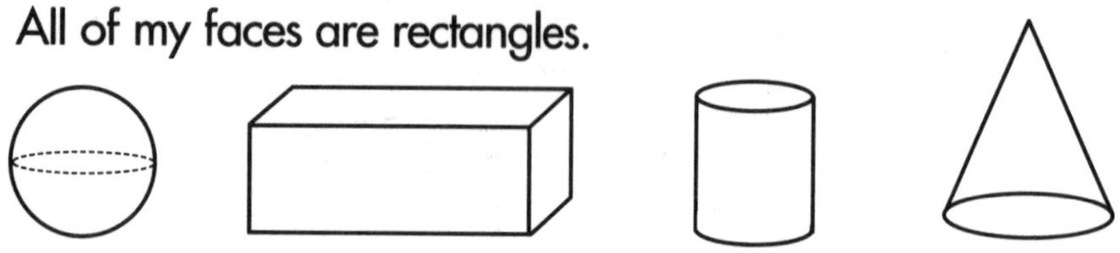

5. I have no edges, no faces, and no vertices.

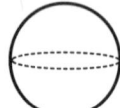 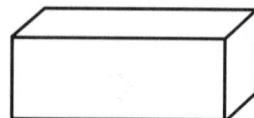  

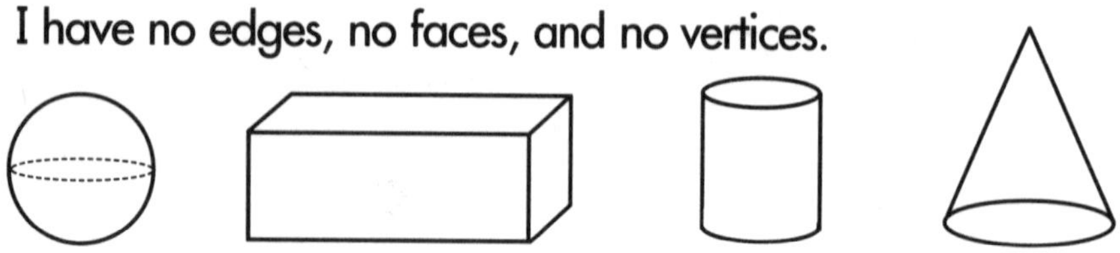

DO MORE

 Write a problem like the ones above to share with a friend.

Stacking Solid Objects

Directions: Use the letters of each solid figure to write an order in which they can be stacked.

1. bottom _____ middle _____ top _____

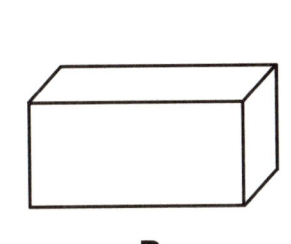

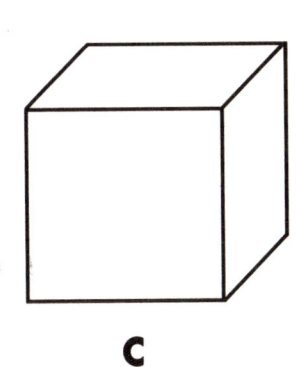

   A   B   C

2. bottom _____ middle _____ top _____

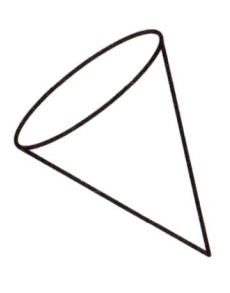

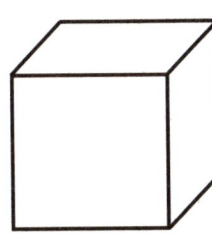

   A   B   C

Relationships

Name _____ Date _____

Will It Roll?

Directions: Circle the word that best tells the possibility of each solid figure rolling.

1. [rectangular prism]   sometimes / always / never

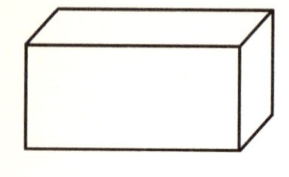

2. [cone]   sometimes / always / never

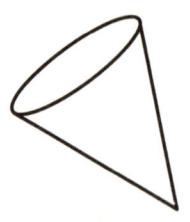

3. [pyramid]   sometimes / always / never

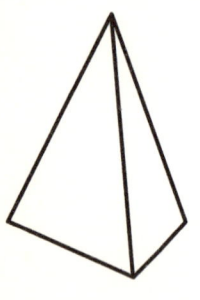

4. [cylinder]   sometimes / always / never

5. [cube]   sometimes / always / never

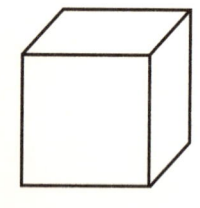

6. [sphere]   sometimes / always / never

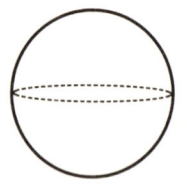

DO MORE

Name a real object that always rolls.

Name a real object that sometimes rolls.

Name a real object that never rolls.

Create Your Own Problems

1. Write a word problem about drawing a specific quadrilateral.

2. Write a question about a solid figure and the number of edges and vertices it has.

3. Write a question about identifying a triangle as equilateral, isosceles, or scalene.

4. Draw a trapezoid. Write a question about a line of symmetry.

Relationships   Name _____   Date _____

Check Your Skills

1. Draw a parallelogram. Tell how you know it is a parallelogram.

_____

_____

2. Draw a figure that is a polygon. Then draw a figure that is not a polygon.

3. How many sides does a pentagon have?

_____

4. What is the name of the solid figure below? Circle the correct answer.

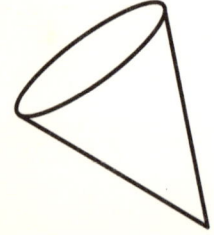

cone

cube

cylinder

Check Your Skills (cont.)

5. How many faces does a rectangular prism have?

   _____

6. Does a sphere have a flat surface?

   _____

7. Is the figure at the right regular or irregular?

   _____

8. Name one solid figure that meets both of these descriptions.
   - six faces that are all squares
   - can have other solid figures stacked on top of it

   _____

9. Draw a hexagon.

Locations

Name _____ Date _____

The Toy Chest

Directions: Fill in each blank with the word **right** or **left**.

| airplane | sailboat | doll | blocks | book |

1. The doll is _____ of the book.

2. The sailboat is _____ of the airplane.

3. The book is _____ of the blocks.

4. The blocks are _____ of the sailboat.

5. The sailboat is _____ of the doll.

6. The airplane is _____ of the book.

THINK

In the picture of the blocks, tell where the N block is to the R block.

42

Published by Instructional Fair. Copyright protected.

0-7424-2982-2 Using the Standards: Geometry

Locations

Three Letter Words

Directions: Follow each instruction to write a three letter word.

1. Write t on the left side of o.
   Write o on the right side of o.

   o

2. Write j on the left side o.
   Write y on the right side of o.

   o

3. Write h on the left side of a.
   Write t on the right side of a.

   a

4. Write a on the right side of s.
   Write y on the right side of a.

   s

5. Write r on the left side of m.
   Write a on the left side of r.

   m

6. Write j on the left side of e.
   Write t on the right side of e.

   e

DO MORE

Write a question of your own using the letter i.

i

Above and Below

Directions: Draw the figure named in each place named.

1. square below the circle

2. triangle above the V

3. rectangle above the square

4. trapezoid below the apple

5. the letter M with a circle below it

6. the letter T with a rhombus above it

Locations

Name _____ Date _____

Going Shopping

Directions: Locate each item on the shelves below.
Circle the words that best describe its place.

1.  🍌 is right of / is left of 🧢(beanie)

2.  🌐 is above / is under 📅

3.  ⛵ is right of / is left of ✈️

4.  🦆 is above / is under 🥜(peanut butter)

5.  🍇 is right of / is left of 🧢(cap)

6.  🧢(cap) is above / is under (blender)

Locations

Sunny or Cloudy

Directions: Draw a sun or clouds to follow each direction.

1. Draw a sun above the clouds.

2. Draw a sun below the clouds.

3. Draw 3 clouds above the sun.

4. Draw 4 clouds below the sun.

Locations

Name _____ Date _____

Study Time

Directions: Draw the books in each picture to match the words.

1. Draw 1 book on the bed.
   Draw 3 books off the bed.

2. Draw 4 books on the desk.
   Draw 2 books off the desk.

DO MORE

Tell how many books you drew in all.

Locations

Name _____ Date _____

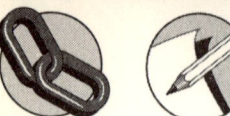

In the Fish Bowl

Directions: Follow each direction.

1. Draw 3 fish inside the bowl.

2. Draw 5 rocks outside the bowl.

3. Draw 1 can of food outside the bowl.

4. Draw 2 more fish inside the bowl.

THINK

How many fish are inside of the fish bowl in question 4?

Published by Instructional Fair. Copyright protected.

0-7424-2982-2 Using the Standards: Geometry

Locations

Name _____ Date _____

In Full Bloom

Directions: Use the grid on page 50 to create a picture.

1. Color each of these blocks yellow.

   J15   K15   K16   J16   I16   I17

   J17   K17

2. Color each of these blocks green.

   A1   B1   C1   D1   E1   F1

   G1   H1   I1   J1   K1   E2

   E3   E4   E5   E6   E7   E8

   F2   H4   G4   G5   H5

3. Color each of these blocks red.

   D9   E9   F9   G10   F10   E10

   D10 C10 G11 F11   E11   D11

   C11 G12 F12 E12   D12   C12

   G13 F13 E13 D13   C13   C14

   E14 G14

4. Name and color five blocks to create another leaf on the left side of the stem.

   ____ ____ ____ ____ ____

49

Published by Instructional Fair. Copyright protected.

0-7424-2982-2 Using the Standards: Geometry

Locations

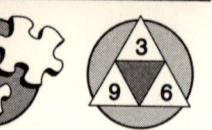

Name _____ Date _____

In Full Bloom

Directions: Color in blocks given on page 49.

Locations

Name _____ Date _____

Directions to a Word

Directions: Follow each direction. Write the letter of the point in each blank.

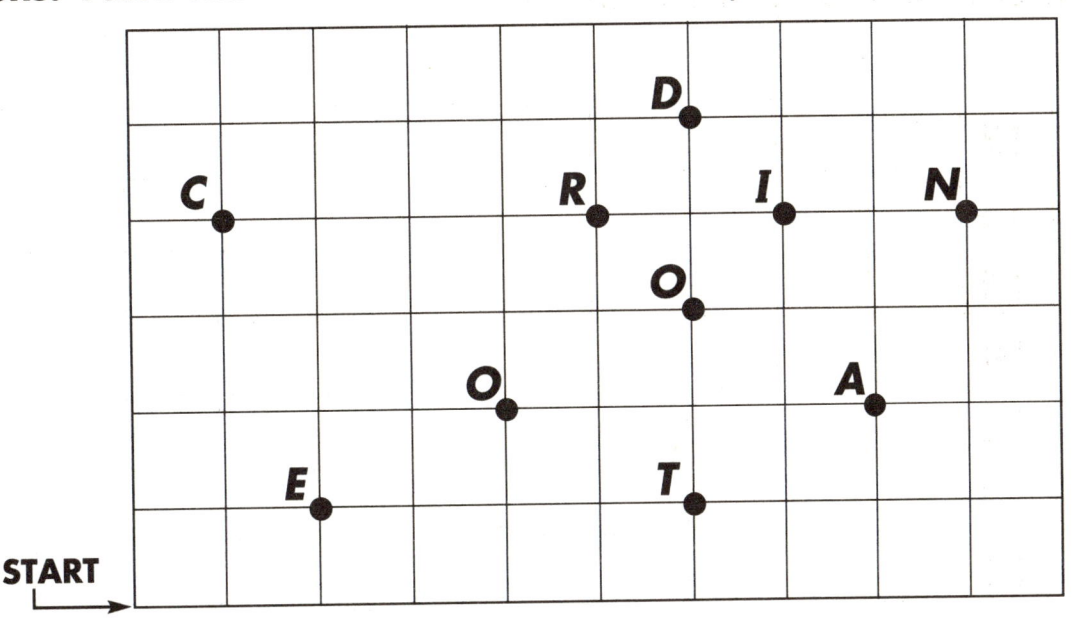

[Grid with points labeled: C, D, R, I, N, O, O, A, E, T, with START arrow at bottom left pointing right]

1. From **START**, go right 1 and up 4. Write the letter. _____
2. From that point, go right 3 and down 2. Write the letter. _____
3. Then, go right 2 and up 1. Write the letter. _____
4. From that point, go left 1 and up 1. Write the letter. _____
5. Next, go right 1 and up 1. Write the letter. _____
6. Now, go down 1 and right 1. Write the letter. _____
7. Next, go right 2. Write the letter. _____
8. Next, go down 2 and left 1. Write the letter. _____
9. Next, go down 1 and left 2. Write the letter. _____
10. Finally, go left 4. Write the letter. _____

What type of grid is used in math? _____

Locations

Name _____ Date _____

About the Town

Directions: Use the map to answer each question.

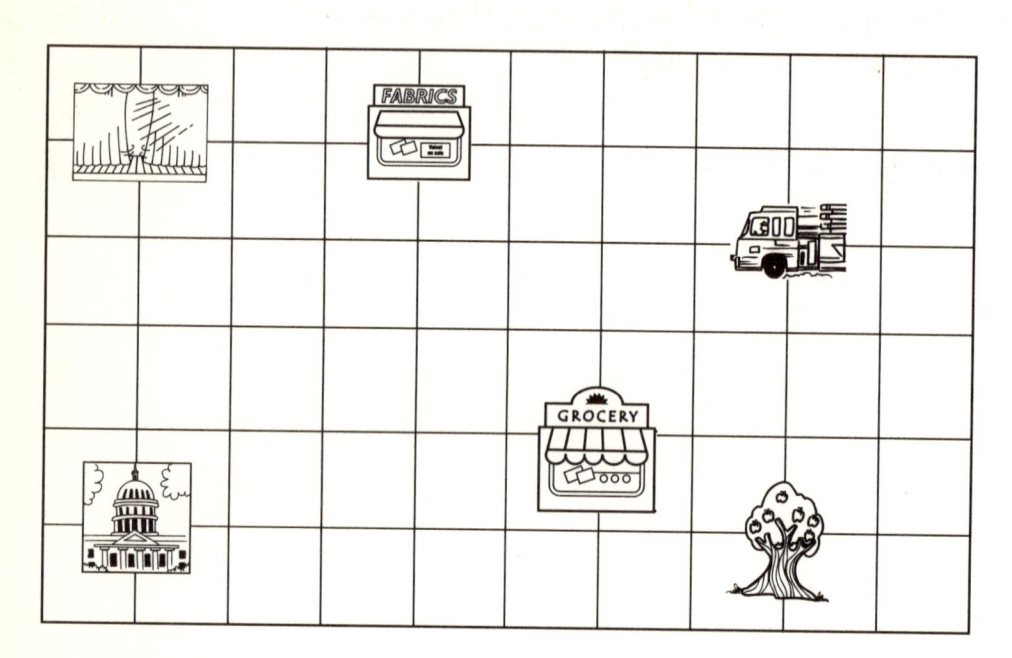

[Map grid showing locations with legend: Fabric Store, Fire Station, Government Building, Grocery, Orchard, Theater]

1. How many blocks is the government building from the fire station? _____

2. How many blocks is the theater from the fabric store? _____

3. The orchard is one block down, and how many blocks right from the grocery? _____

4. What place is the fewest blocks from the government building? _____

THINK

Write a question that includes the grocery and the theater.

Locations

Polygon People

Directions: Graph each ordered pair. Start at 0.
Move the first number right. Move the second number up.
Connect the points to form a polygon.

Ordered pairs: (2, 2), (6, 3), (4, 6), (0, 5)

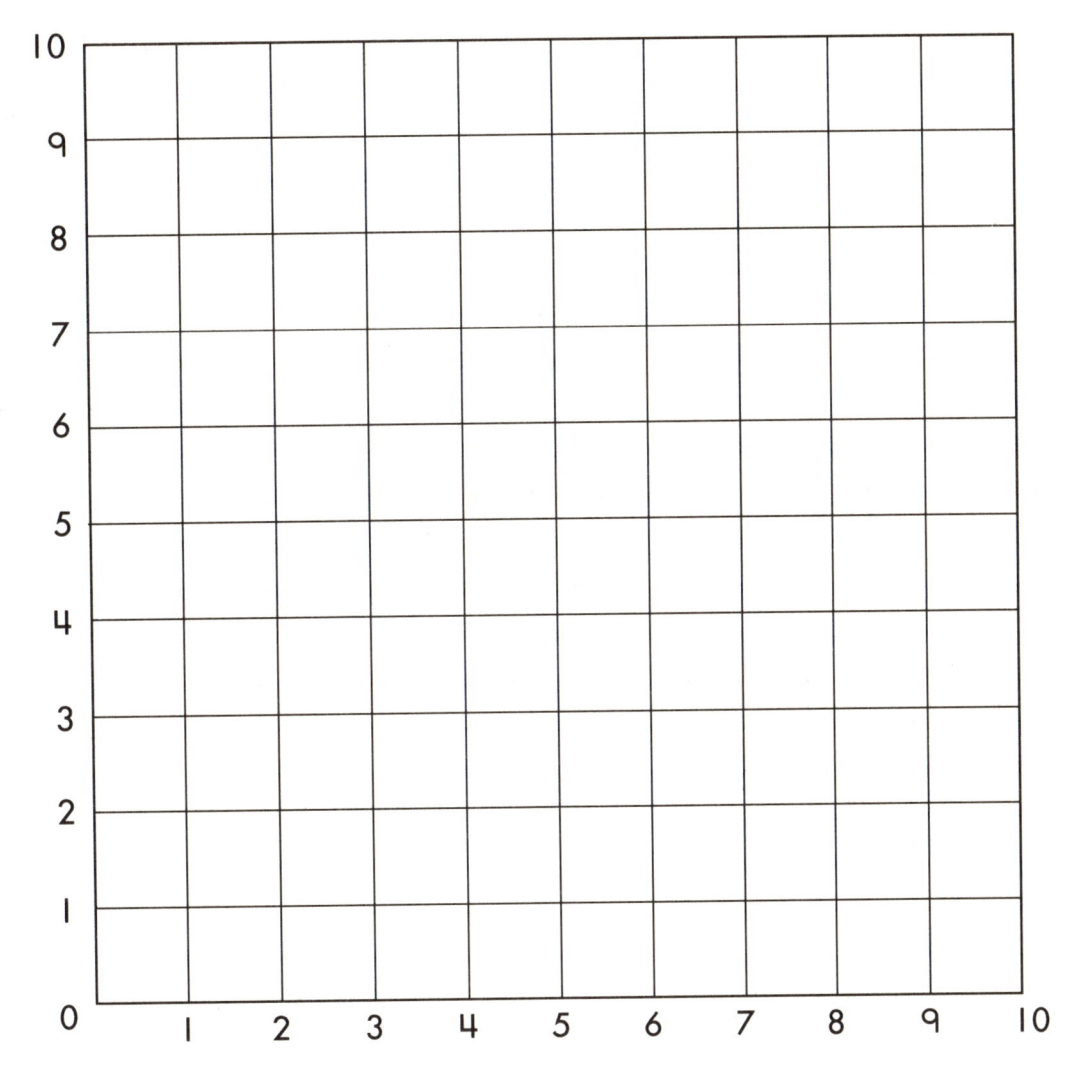

What polygon did you make? _____

Add a face, arms, and legs to make a polygon person.

Locations

End to End

Directions: Name the ordered pairs of the endpoint of each line segment.

1.

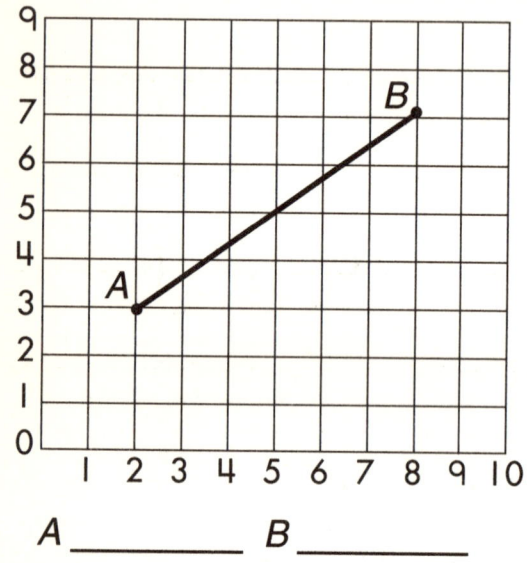

A _____ B _____

2.

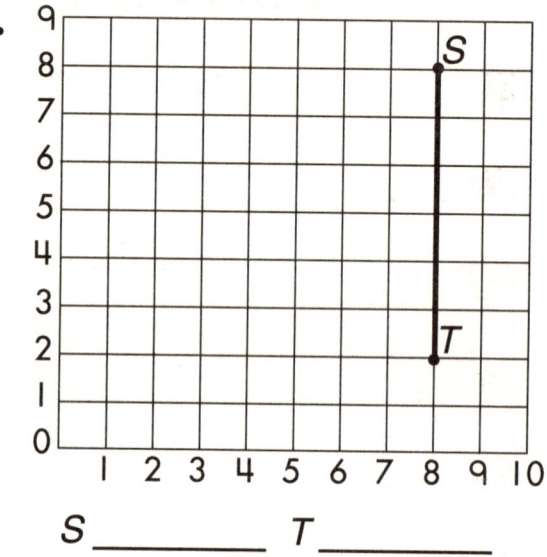

S _____ T _____

3.

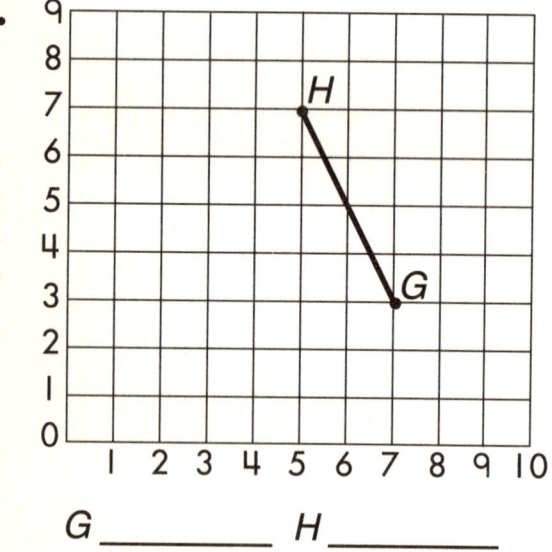

G _____ H _____

4.

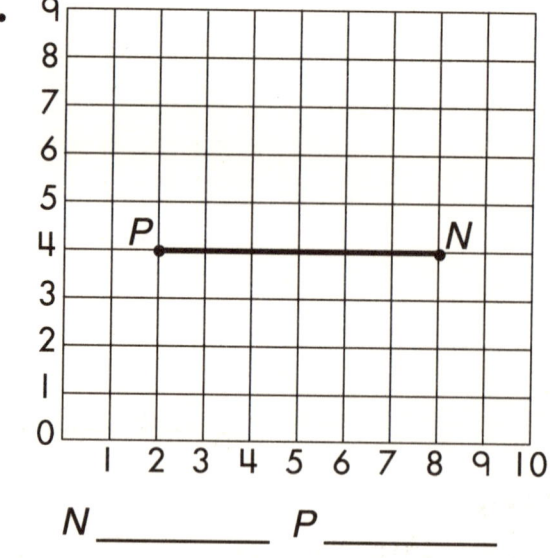

N _____ P _____

THINK

Describe how you found the ordered pair for G in question 3.

Locations

Length of Line Segments

Directions: Find the distance (in units) of each line segment on the coordinate grid.

1. $\overline{AB}$ ____
2. $\overline{FM}$ ____
3. $\overline{PC}$ ____
4. $\overline{JK}$ ____
5. $\overline{TS}$ ____
6. $\overline{BC}$ ____

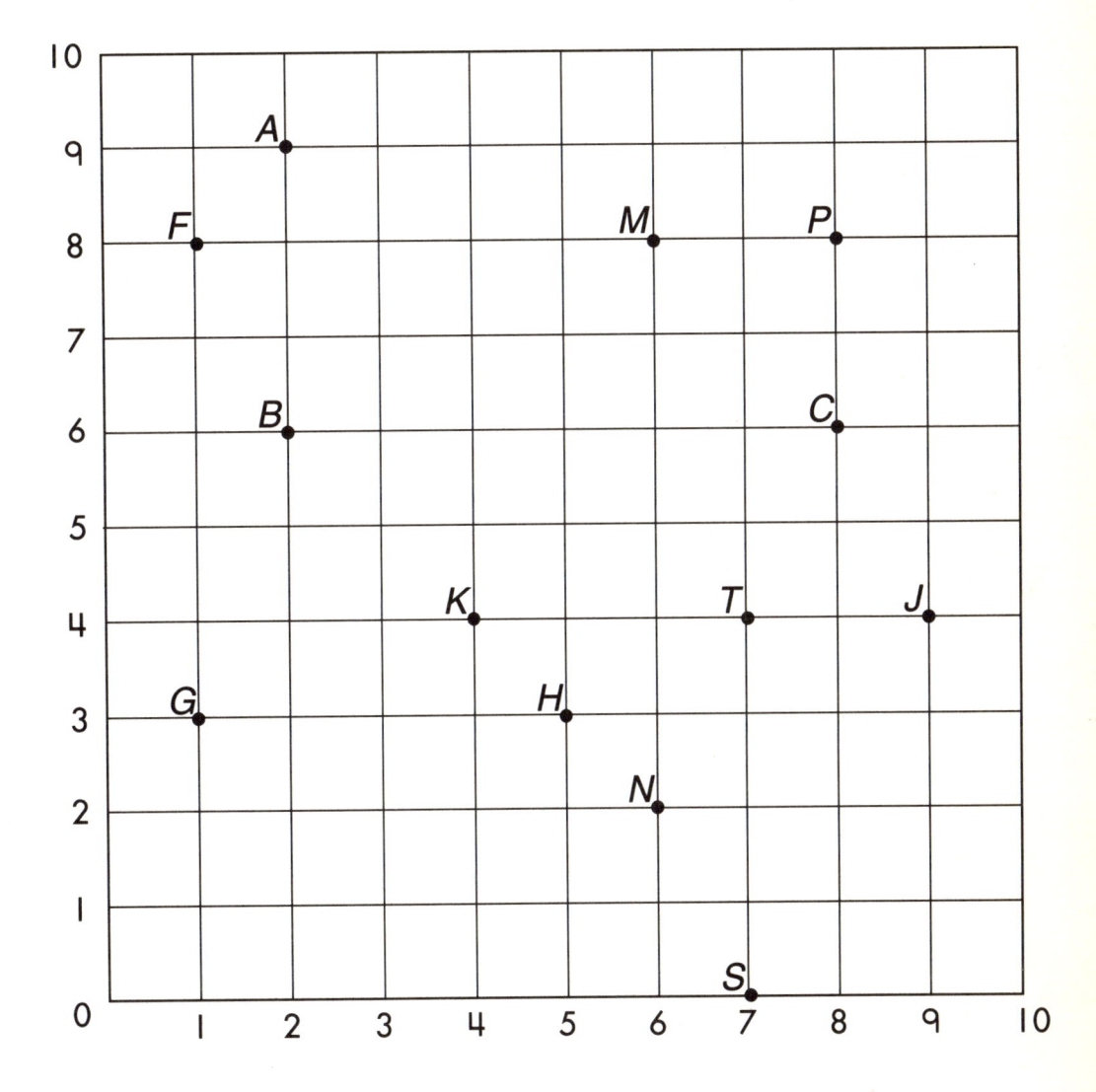

THINK

Draw line segment NQ so that its length is 6 units. Plot the point Q, and name its ordered pair.

Locations

Name _____ Date _____

Plot for Distance

Directions: Graph a point to make each horizontal line segment.

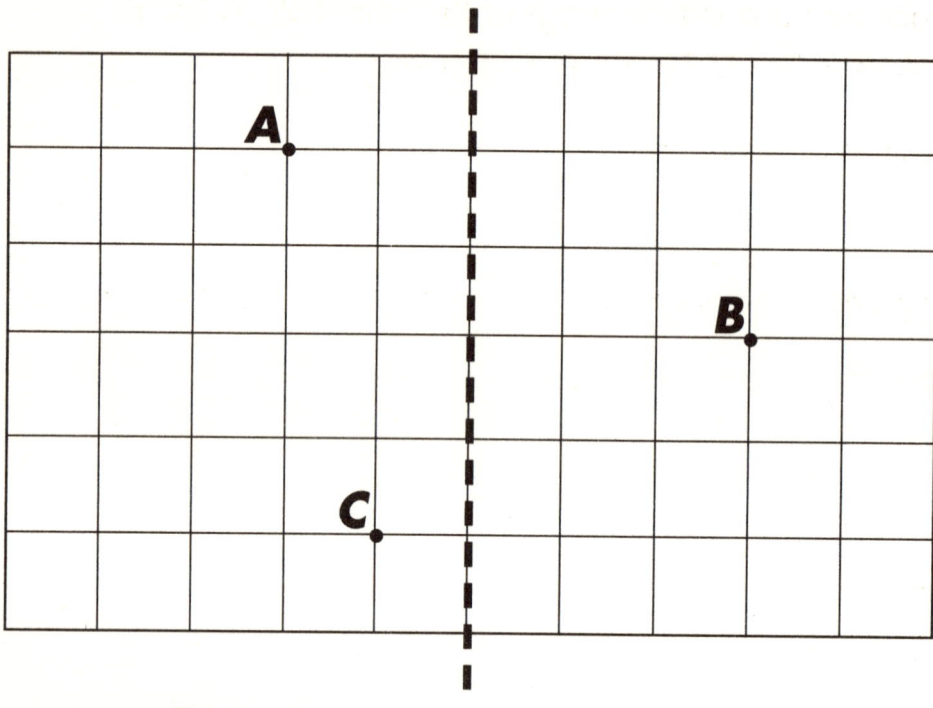

1. Plot point D so that $\overline{AD}$ is 4 units long.

2. Plot point E so that $\overline{BE}$ is 7 units long.

3. Plot point O so that $\overline{CO}$ is 5 units long.

4. Plot point W so that $\overline{WE}$ is 2 units long.

5. Plot point R so that $\overline{RO}$ is 3 units long.

THINK

Which letters are mirror images of each other when you view the dotted rule as a line of symmetry?

Lines of Symmetry

A **line of symmetry** is a line that divides a picture or shape into two equal halves. Each half is a mirror image of the other half. A line of symmetry can be vertical, horizontal, or diagonal.

A square has 4 lines of symmetry.

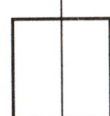

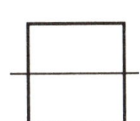

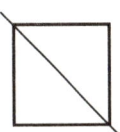

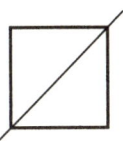

Directions: Is the line a line of symmetry for each figure? Circe the correct answer.

1. 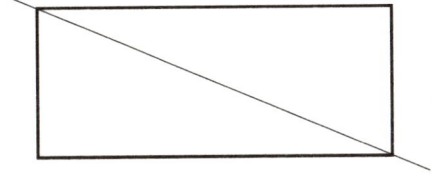   yes   no

2. 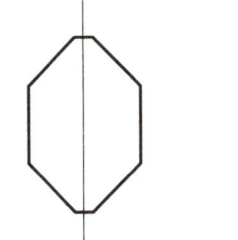   yes   no

3. 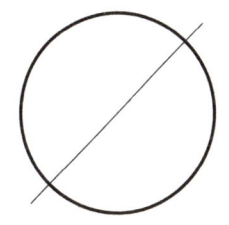   yes   no

4. 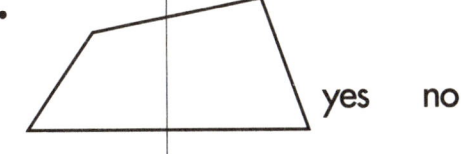   yes   no

5. 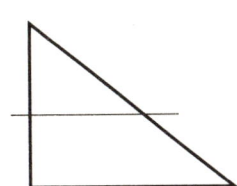   yes   no

6. 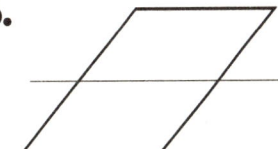   yes   no

DO MORE

Choose a figure you answered "no" to and draw a line of symmetry.

Locations

Picture of Symmetry

Directions: The points on the left side of a picture are shown. The picture has a line of symmetry shown with a dotted rule. Place the points on the right half of the picture. Connect the points to draw the picture.

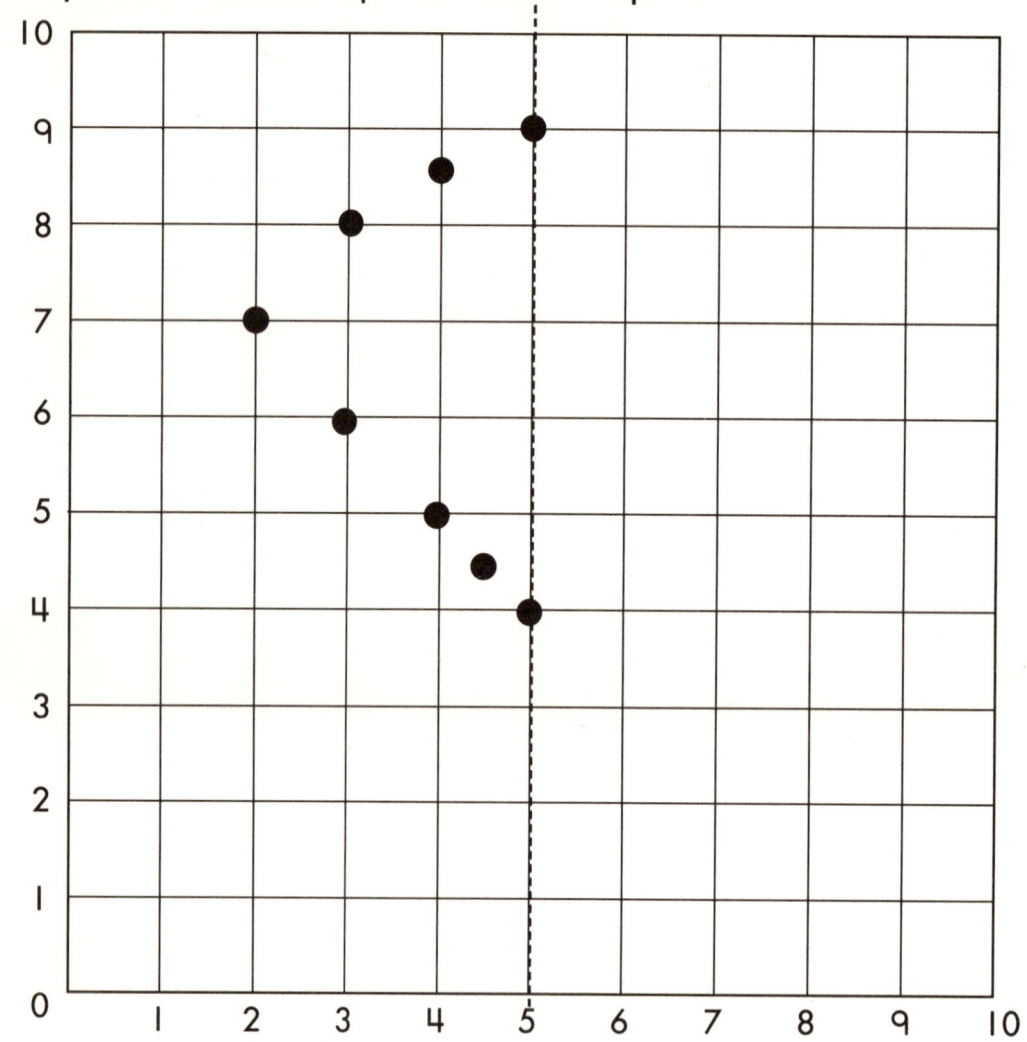

Name the ordered pairs you can graph to add a tail to your picture.

1. _____   2. _____   3. _____   4. _____

5. _____   6. _____   7. _____   8. _____

Two Lines of Symmetry

Directions: On each figure below, draw 2 lines of symmetry.

1.

2.

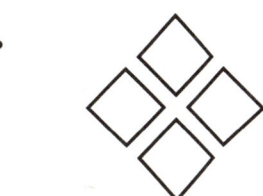

3.

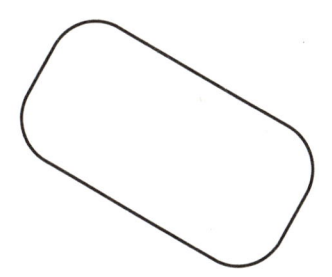

4.

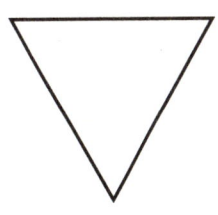

5.

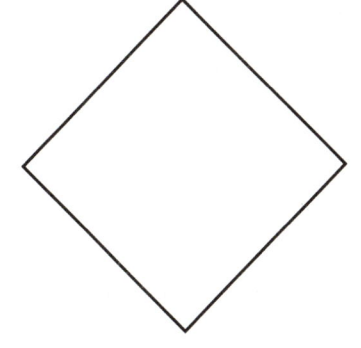

6.

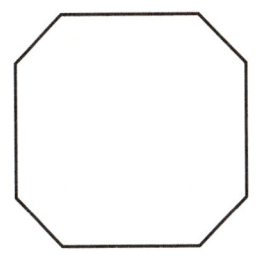

Locations

Draw with Symmetry

Directions: Use the dotted rule as a line of symmetry. Complete the figure so that it has symmetry.

1.

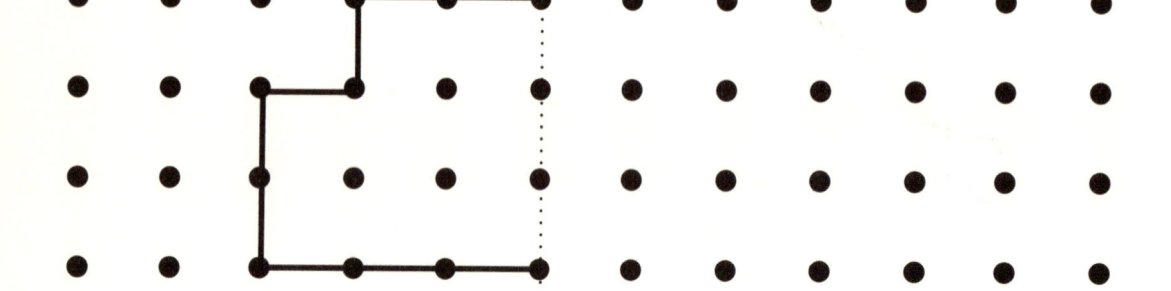

2.

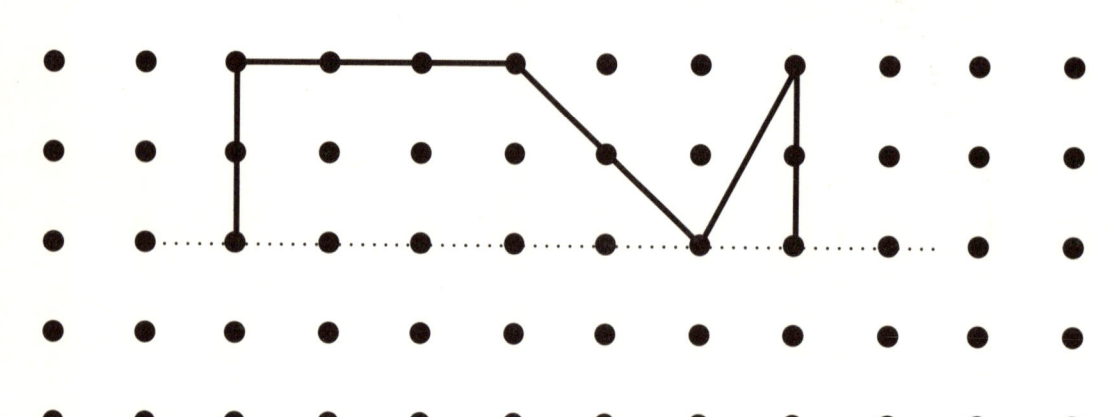

Locations

More Pictures with Symmetry

Directions: Use the dotted rule as a line of symmetry.
Complete the figure so that it has symmetry.
Name each object.

1.

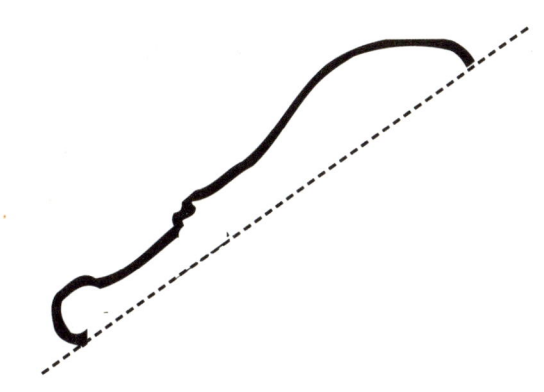

2.

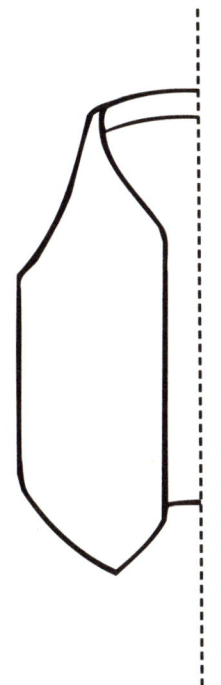

Locations

Create Your Own Problems

1. Write a question about naming the ordered pair of a point on a coordinate grid.

2. Draw a half of a square on a coordinate grid. Write a question about completing the drawing.

3. Write a word. Then write a question about naming a letter right of another letter.

4. Write a question about a line of symmetry drawn through a picture of a heart.

Locations

Check Your Skills

Use the coordinate grid below for questions 1 and 3.

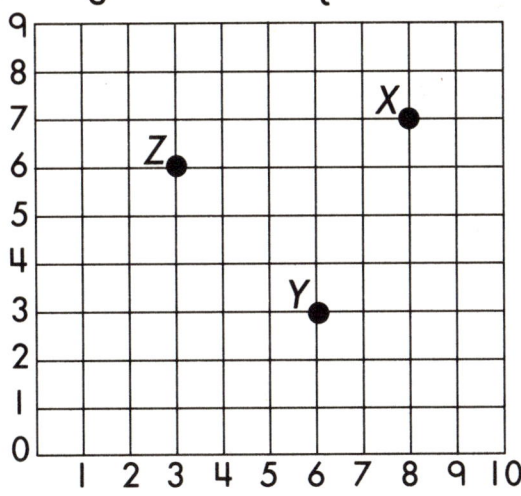

1. Name the coordinates of each point.

   X: _____   Y: _____

   Z: _____

2. Graph a fourth point so that the figure is a parallelogram. Name the ordered pair of the point. Connect the points to show your parallelogram.

   _____

3. Write a sentence to tell where point X is compared to point Y using one of the following words.

   right   left   above   below

   _____

Locations

Check Your Skills (cont.)

4. Tell if the line shown is a line of symmetry. Circle the correct answer.

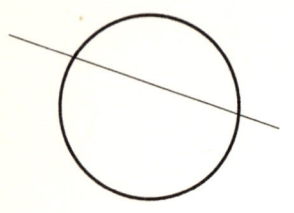

   yes

   no

5. Draw a figure that does not have a line of symmetry.

6. Draw a cloud above the house and grass below the house.

Flips

A flip creates a mirror image.

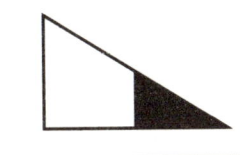

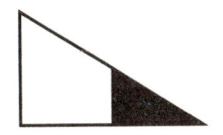

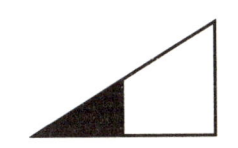

horizontal flip

vertical flip

Directions: Is the image on the right a horizontal flip or a vertical flip of the image on the left? Circle the correct answer.

1. horizontal   vertical

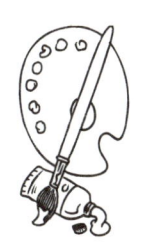

2. horizontal   vertical

3. horizontal   vertical

4. horizontal   vertical

Transformations

Name _____ Date _____

Slides

A **slide** creates the same image in a different location.

Directions: Is the image on the right a slide of the image on the left? Circle yes or no.

1. 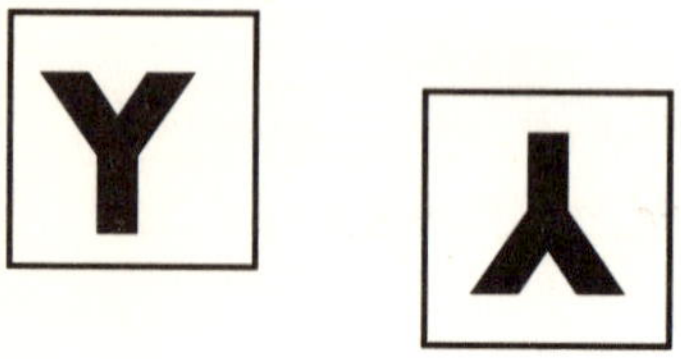 yes   no

2.  yes   no

3.  yes   no

4. 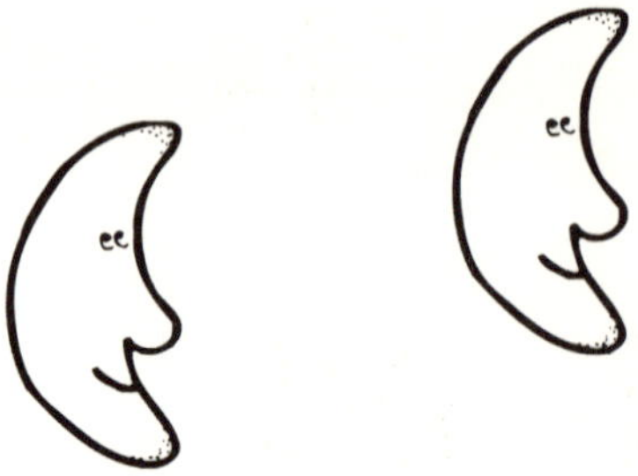 yes   no

THINK

Describe the direction of any slides in questions 1 – 4.

Turns in Both Directions

A → A clockwise turn

A ← A counterclockwise turn

Directions: Decide if each turn is clockwise or counterclockwise. Circle the correct answer.

1. clockwise   counterclockwise

2. clockwise   counterclockwise

3. clockwise   counterclockwise

4. clockwise   counterclockwise

5. clockwise   counterclockwise

DO MORE

Write the number 7. Show it turned clockwise. Then show it turned counterclockwise.

Show a Flip, Slide, and Turn

Directions: Draw each image. Then draw the image as a flip, slide, and turn.

1. a circle with one-half colored red

   image   flip   slide   turn

2. a square with one-fourth colored blue

   image   flip   slide   turn

3. a trapezoid with the number 2 inside

   image   flip   slide   turn

Transformations

A **transformation** creates a new image from an original image.

A **flip** is a transformation that creates a mirror image of the original image.

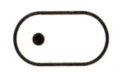

A **slide** is a transformation that creates an image moved from the location of the original image.

A **turn** is a transformation that creates a rotated image of the original image.

Directions: Draw what each image looks like when the named transformation is applied.

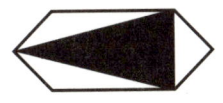

1. slide

2. turn (quarter turn counterclockwise)

3. turn (quarter turn clockwise)

4. flip

5. slide

Transformations   Name _____   Date _____

Match the Transformation

Directions: Circle the picture that shows the named transformation.

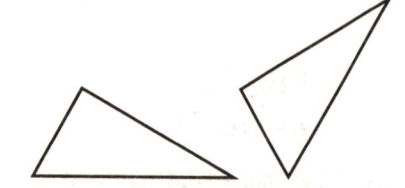

1. turn

2. flip

3. slide

4. turn

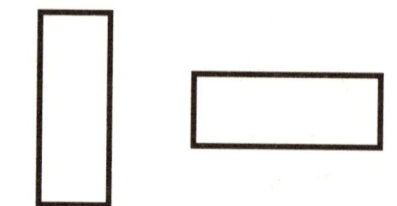

DO MORE

Draw an original figure. Then draw a transformation of that figure.

Transformations

Transform Pattern Blocks

Directions: Use pattern blocks. Flip and slide each block. Then complete the chart below, and on page 72, by drawing how each block looks. If the vertical flip looks the same as the horizontal flip, write "same" in the vertical flip column.

Pattern Block	Flip it. (horizontal)	Flip it. (vertical)	Slide it.
1. square			
2. triangle			
3. rhombus			

Transformations

Name _____ Date _____

Transform Pattern Blocks

Directions: Use pattern blocks. Flip and slide each block. Then complete the chart below as you did on page 71. If the vertical flip looks the same as the horizontal flip, write "same" in the vertical flip column.

Pattern Block	Flip it. (horizontal)	Flip it. (vertical)	Slide it.
4. parallelogram			
5. hexagon			
6. trapezoid			

Transformations

Name _____ Date _____

More Block Transformations

Directions: Use pattern blocks. Turn each block. Then complete the chart below, and on page 74, by drawing how each block looks. If the clockwise turn looks the same as the counterclockwise turn, write "same" in the counterclockwise column.

Pattern Block	Turn it. ↷ (clockwise)	Turn it. ↶ (counterclockwise)
1. square		
2. triangle		
3. rhombus		

73

Published by Instructional Fair. Copyright protected.

0-7424-2982-2 Using the Standards: Geometry

Transformations

Name _____ Date _____

More Block Transformations

Directions: Use pattern blocks. Turn each block. Then complete the chart below as you did on page 73. If the clockwise turn looks the same as the counterclockwise turn write "same" in the counterclockwise column.

Pattern Block	Turn it. (clockwise)	Turn it. (counterclockwise)
4. parallelogram		
5. hexagon		
6. trapezoid		

Transformations

Name _____ Date _____

Split in Half?

Directions: Decide if the line shown is a line of symmetry. Circle yes or no.

1.

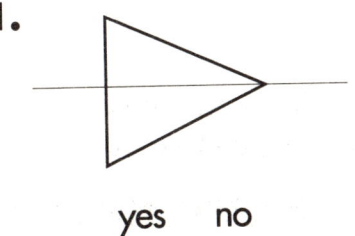

yes   no

2.

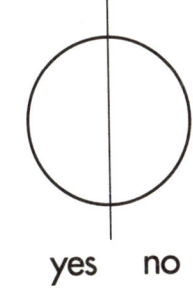

yes   no

3.

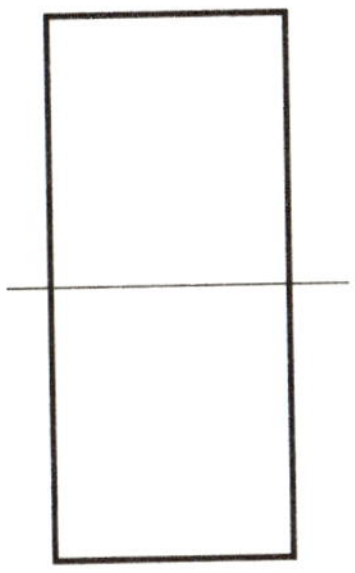

yes   no

4.

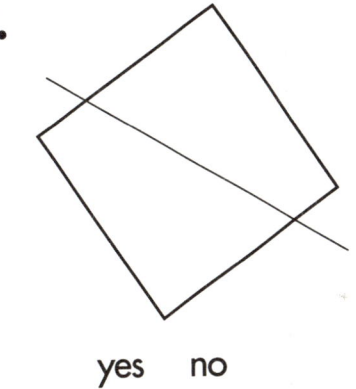

yes   no

5.

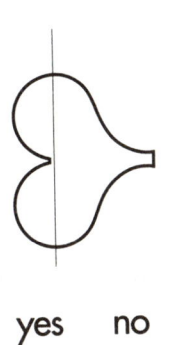

yes   no

6.

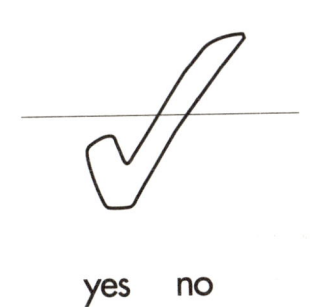

yes   no

THINK

Which shapes above have more than 2 lines of symmetry?

Transformations Name _____ Date _____

Symmetry in the World

Directions: Decide if the line shown on each object is a line of symmetry. Write yes or no.

1. _____

2. _____

3. _____

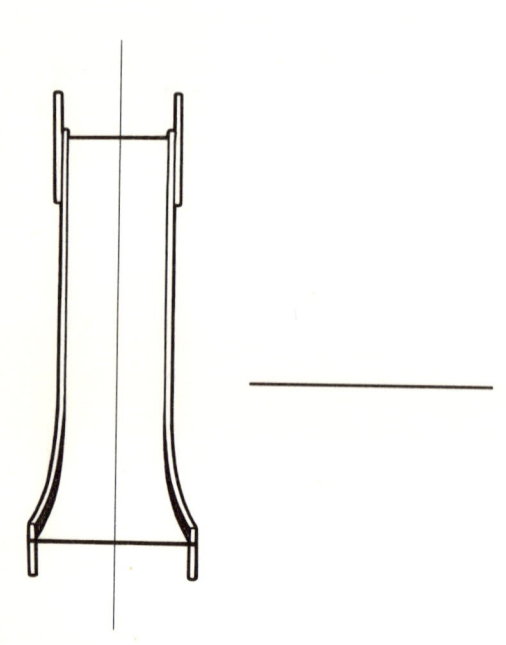

4. _____

THINK

Tell why this line is not a line of symmetry.

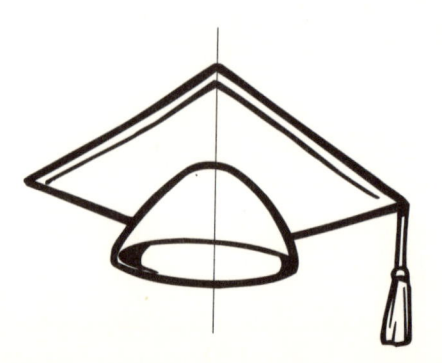

Transformations

Many Lines of Symmetry

Directions: Circle the number of lines of symmetry for each figure shown.

1.  0   1   2   3   4

2.  0   1   2   3   4

3.  0   1   2   3   4

4.  0   1   2   3   4

5.  0   1   2   3   4

6. 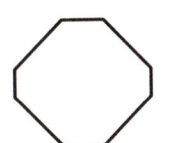 0   1   2   3   4

7. 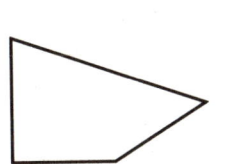 0   1   2   3   4

Point Symmetry

A figure that is turned about a point and looks exactly like itself before one complete rotation (360 degrees) has **point symmetry**.

Point symmetry is also called **rotational symmetry**.

Directions: Use pattern blocks to test if each has point symmetry. Write yes or no.

1.

2.

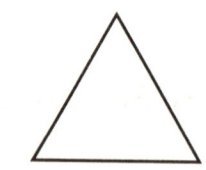

3.

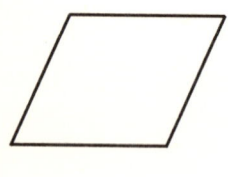

4.

5.

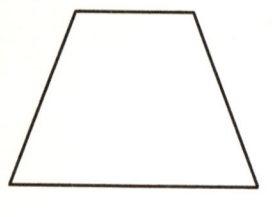

6.

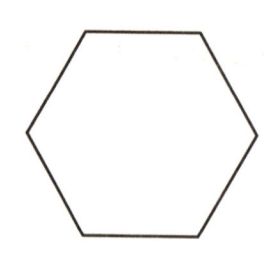

Transformations

Name _____ Date _____

Create Your Own Problems

1. Write a problem that involves one of the pattern blocks and a transformation.

2. Draw an image. Then draw that image transformed. Write a question about the transformation.

3. Write a word problem about how a slide transformation is used when playing on the playground.

4. Make a question about a plane figure that has 2 lines of symmetry.

Transformations

Name _____ Date _____

Check Your Skills

1. Write a number that looks the same in its original position and when it is flipped.

   _____

2. How many lines of symmetry does an isosceles trapezoid have?

   _____

3. Which transformation is shown below?

   _____

4. Draw this image as a flip, slide, and turn (counterclockwise).

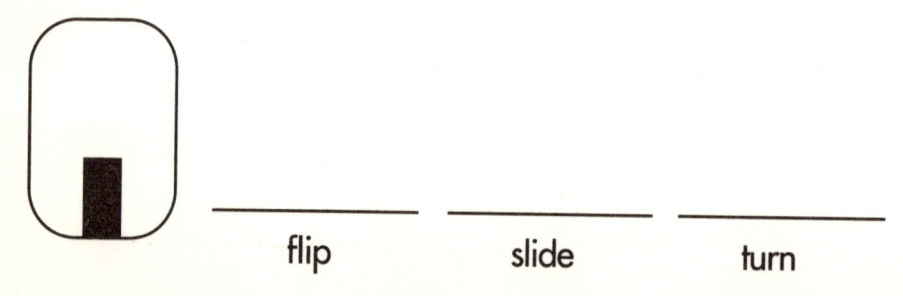

   _____   _____   _____
    flip   slide   turn

Transformations

Check Your Skills (cont.)

5. Sketch the figure below after a vertical flip.

6. How many lines of symmetry are in the figure below? Draw any lines of symmetry.

_____

7. Does the shape below have point symmetry?

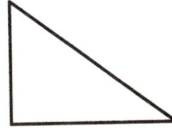

_____

8. Describe how the letter "E" looks after each transformation named.

   a. turned counterclockwise _____

   b. slide to the right _____

Modeling   Name _____   Date _____

Shapes in Your World

Directions: Shapes are all around you. Look around your house or your classroom. Find each of these shapes. Name the object you spotted.

1. square _____

2. trapezoid _____

3. equilateral triangle _____

4. triangle _____

5. rectangle _____

6. pentagon _____

7. right triangle _____

8. hexagon _____

THINK

What shape was the easiest to find?

Solid Figures in Your World

Directions: Solid figures are all around you. Look around your house or your classroom. Find each of these solid figures. Name the object you spotted.

1. cone _____

2. cylinder _____

3. cube _____

4. square pyramid _____

5. rectangular prism _____

6. sphere _____

THINK

For which solid figure could you find the most objects?

Modeling

Name _____ Date _____

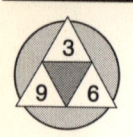

Use Dot Paper to Draw

Directions: Use the dot paper to draw each figure.

1. a square that is 2 units by 2 units

2. a rectangle that is 4 units by 3 units

THINK

Why is dot paper useful for drawing figures?

Modeling

More Dot Paper Drawings

Directions: Use the dot paper to draw each figure.

1. a right triangle that has a height of 5 units and a base of 5 units

2. a parallelogram that has 2 sides 7 units long

THINK

What is another name for the triangle in question 1?

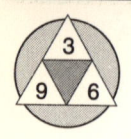

Match Maker

Directions: Draw another shape on the dot paper to match each shape.

1.

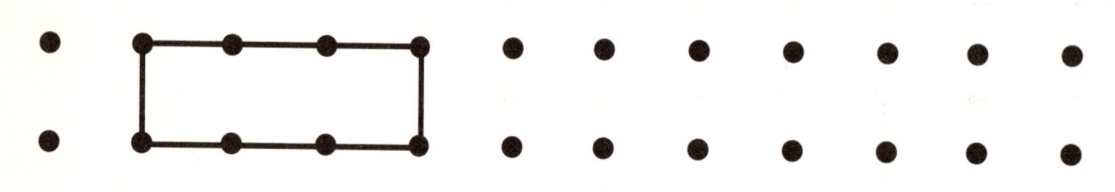

2.

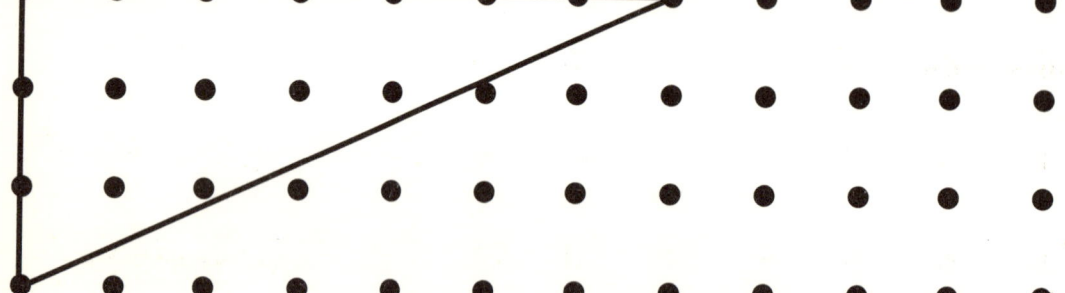

3.

Modeling

Name _____ Date _____

Congruent Shapes

Directions: Are the 2 shapes the same size and the same shape? Circle congruent for yes or not congruent for no.

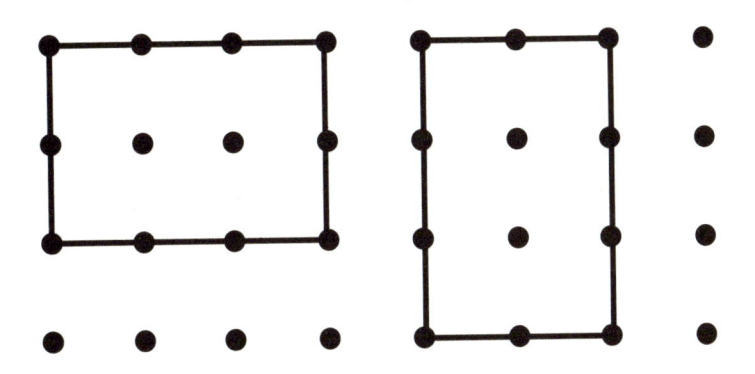

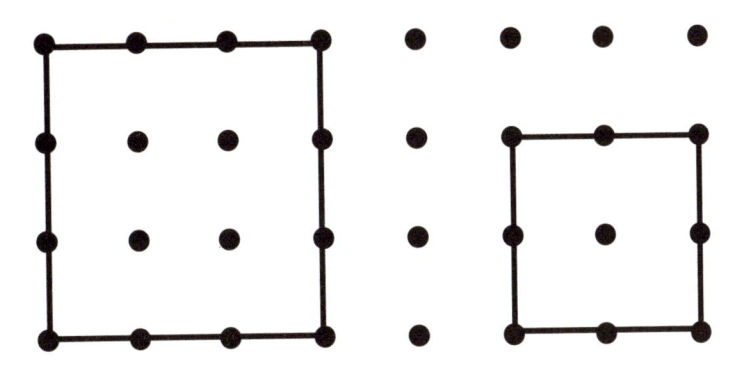

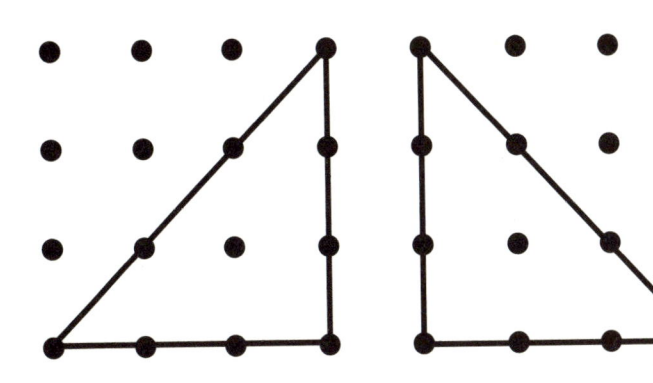

1. congruent

   not congruent

2. congruent

   not congruent

3. congruent

   not congruent

87

Published by Instructional Fair. Copyright protected.

0-7424-2982-2 Using the Standards: Geometry

Perimeters on Dot Paper

Perimeter is the distance around a figure.

Directions: Find the perimeter of each figure. Answer the question.

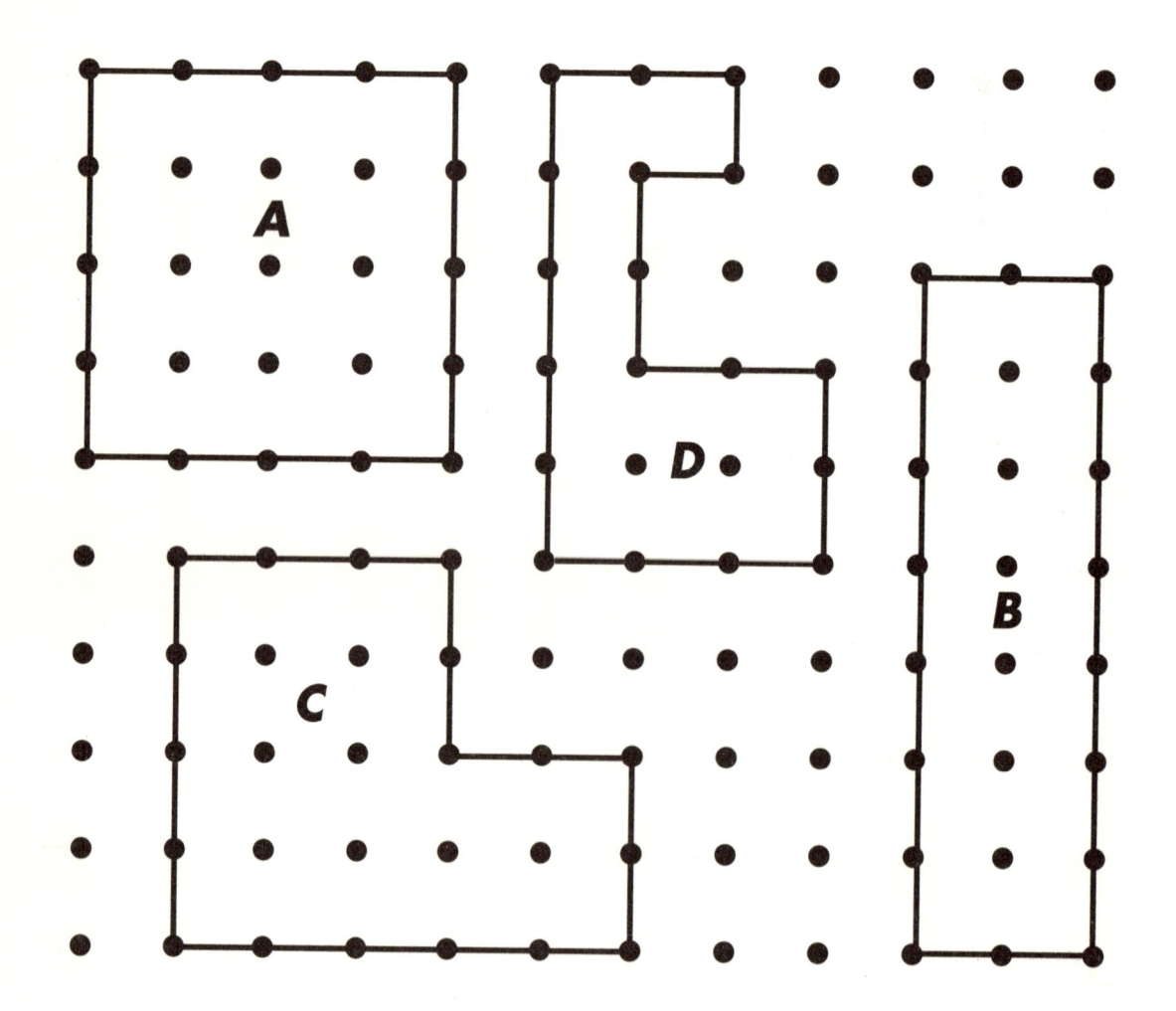

Which figure has a perimeter that is different than the other three figures? _____

Modeling

Name _____ Date _____

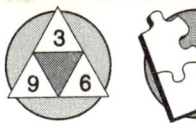

Areas on Dot Paper

Area is the number of square units in the inside of a plane figure.

Directions: Find the area of shape N. Then draw 2 more shapes that have the same area as N.

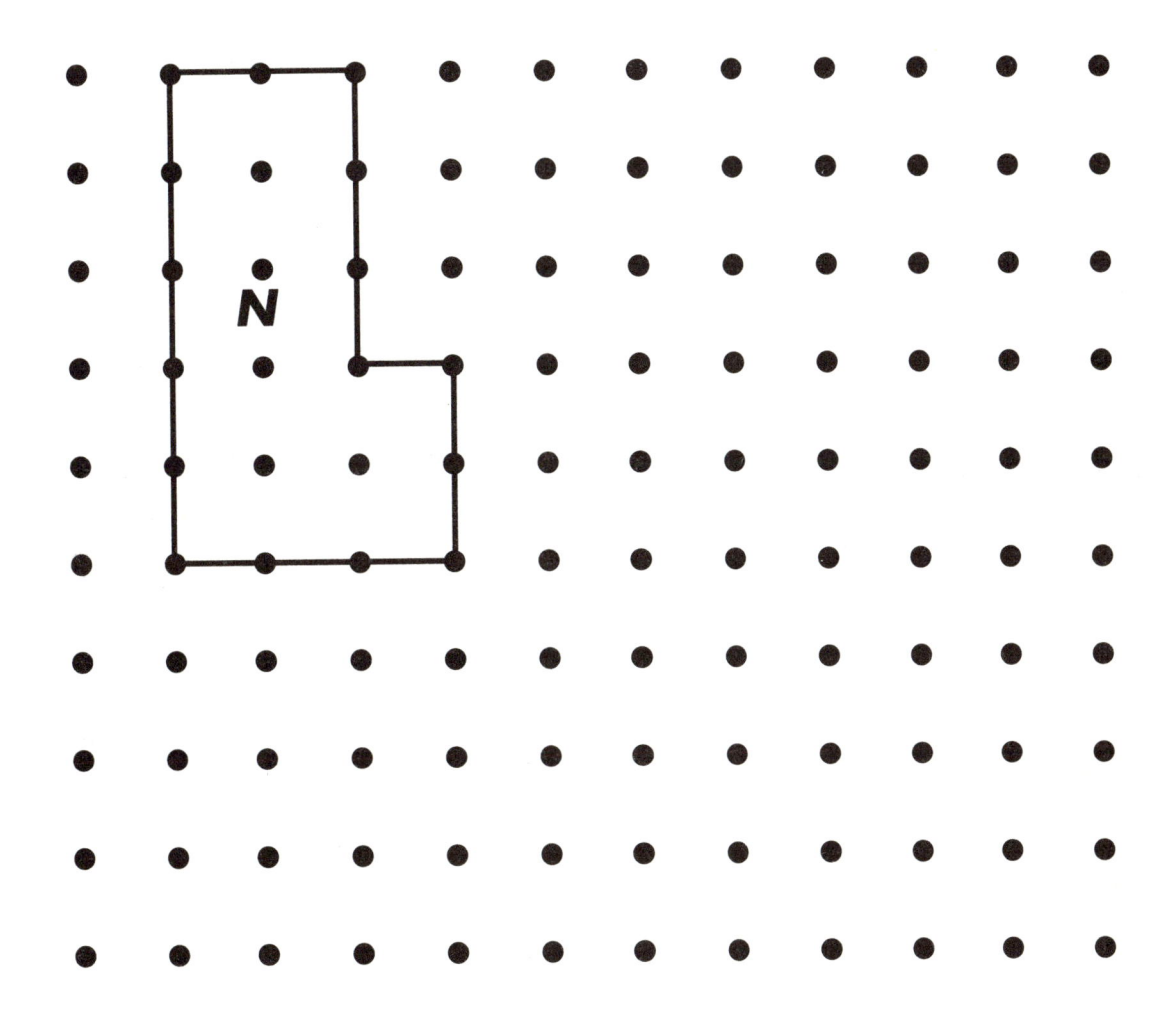

THINK

Can a figure have the same number of units of its perimeter and square units of its area? Tell why.

Modeling

Draw a Cube Using Dot Paper

Directions: Trace the dotted line segments to draw a cube.

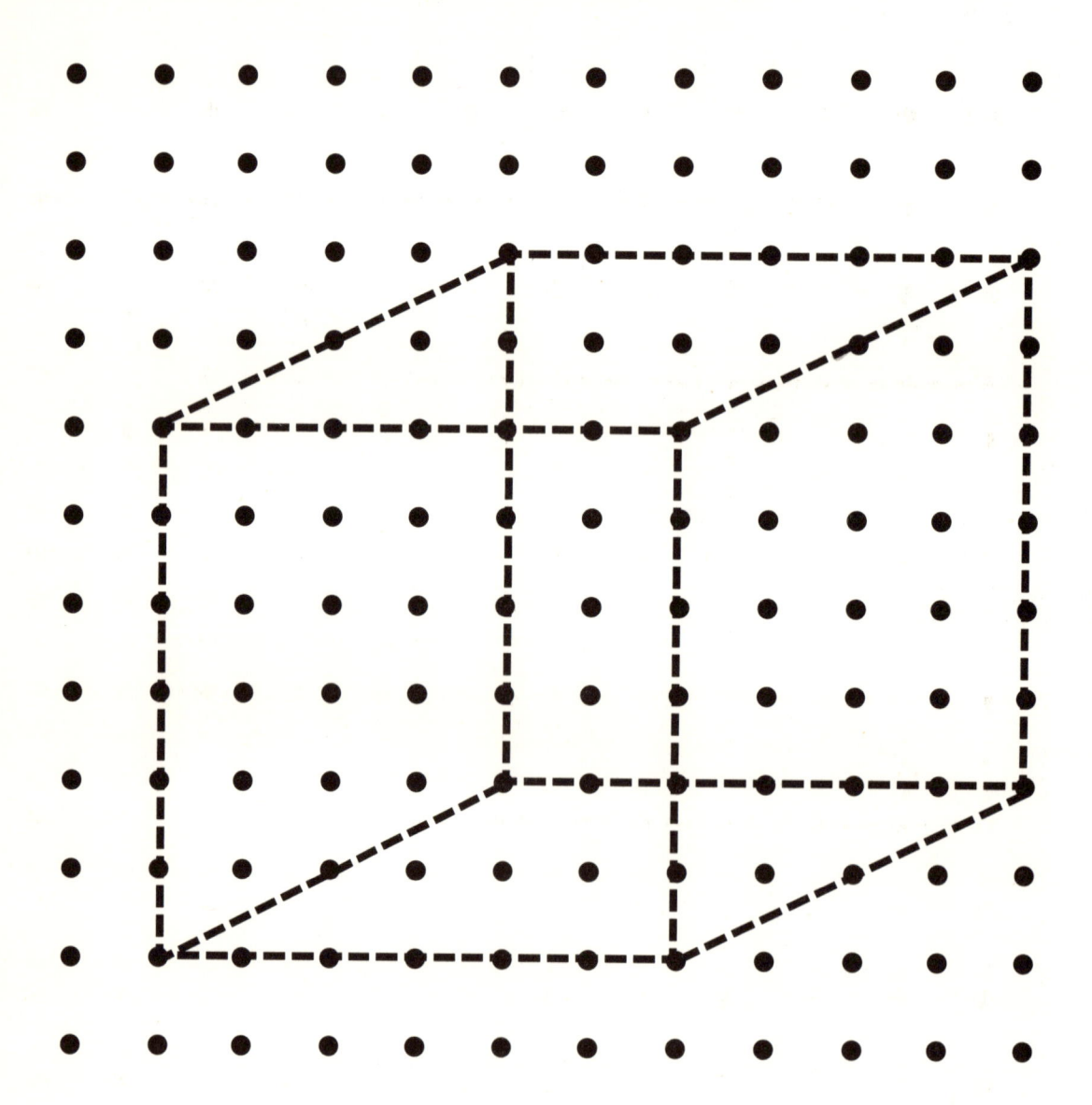

THINK

How many square faces do you see in the cube?

Modeling

Rectangular Prism on Dot Paper

Directions: Trace the dotted line segments to draw a rectangular prism.

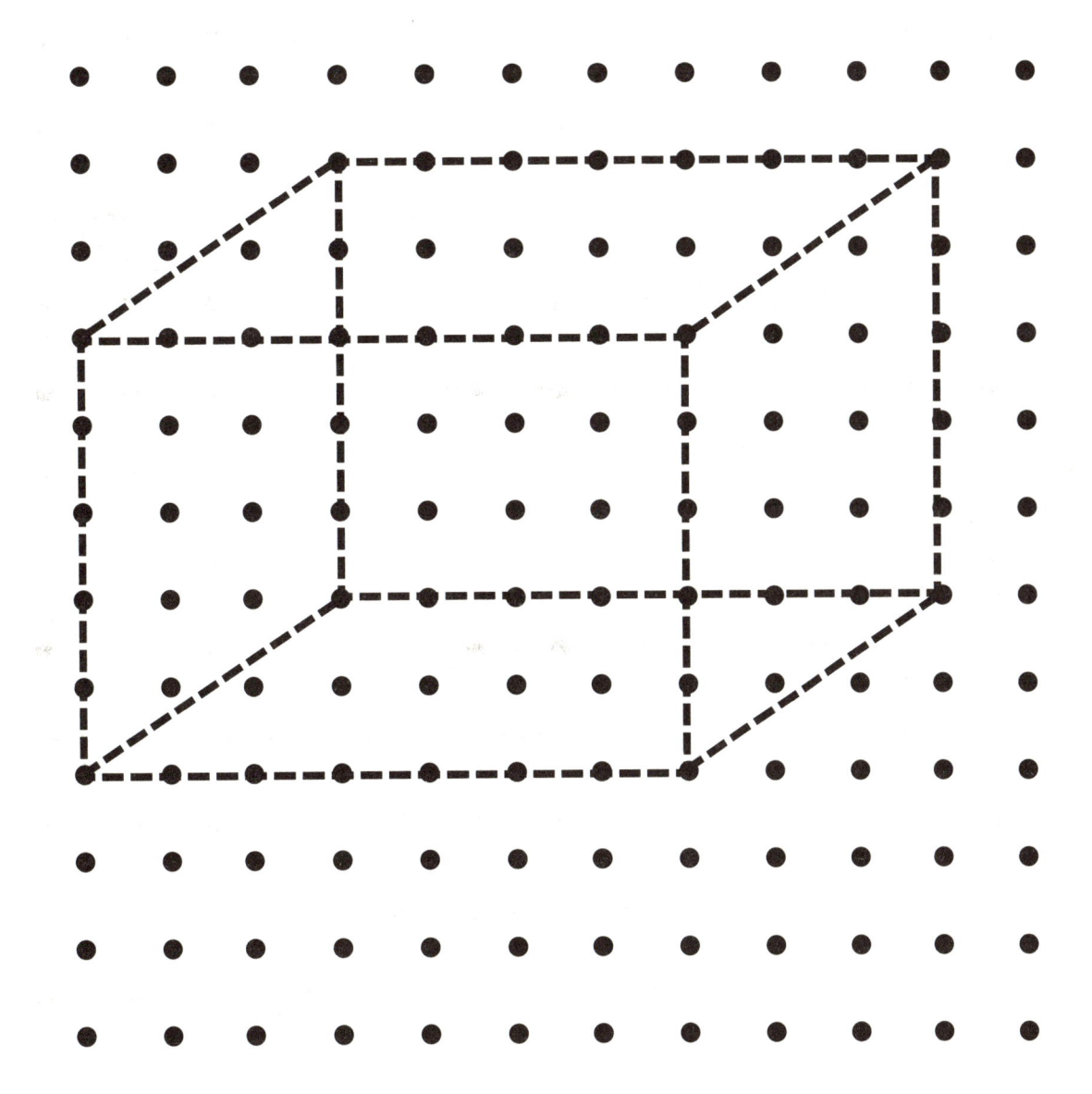

DO MORE

Shade the rectangle that you see as the front face in your drawing.

Modeling

Draw Another Cube

Directions: Trace over the solid line segments to draw the cube. Dashed segments should be traced as dashed segments.

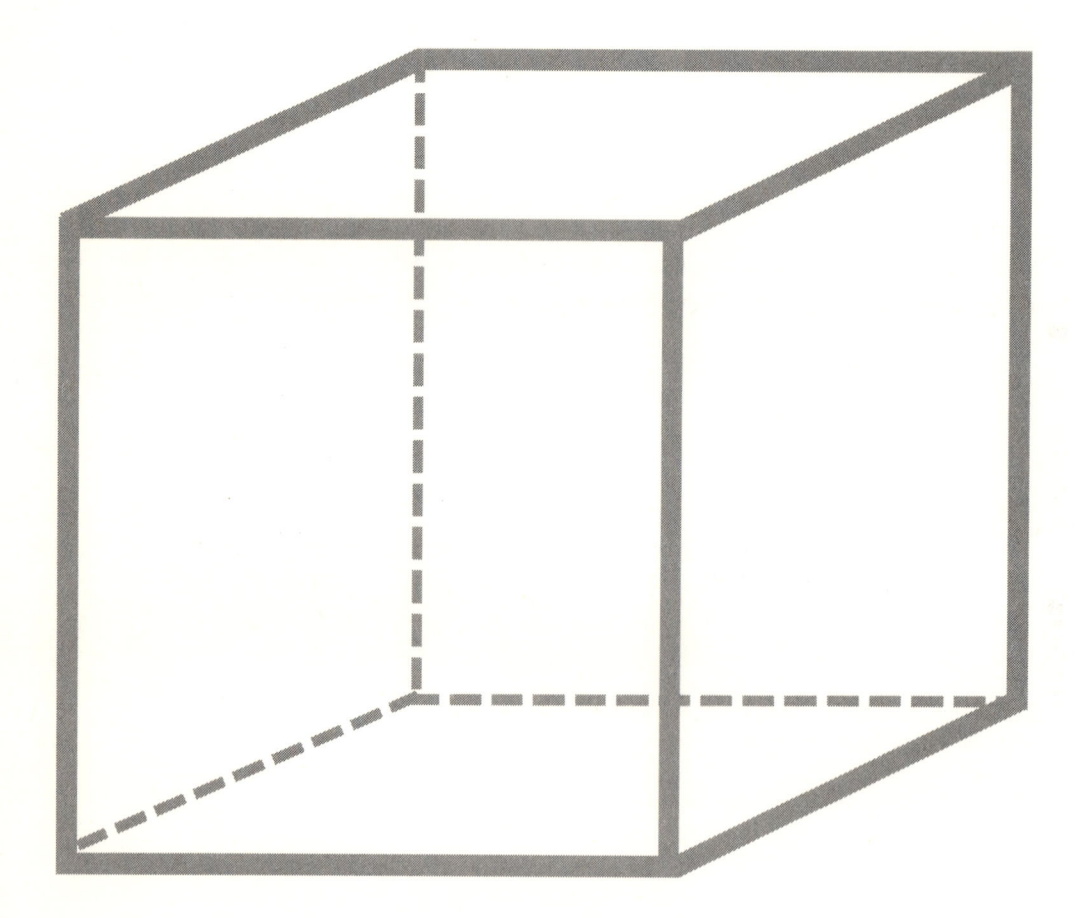

THINK

Why are some of the line segments made with dashed rules?

Draw Another Prism

Directions: Trace over the line segments to draw the front face of a rectangular prism. Then use your drawing from page 92 as a guide to finish drawing the prism.

THINK

What was the first thing you drew after you traced over the rectangle? Why?

Draw a Cylinder

Directions: Trace over the solid line segments and curves to draw each cylinder. Dashed segments and curves should be traced as dashed segments and dashed curves.

THINK

What is the difference between the two cylinders?

Modeling Name _____ Date _____

Draw a Cone

Directions: Trace over the solid line segments and curves to draw the cone.

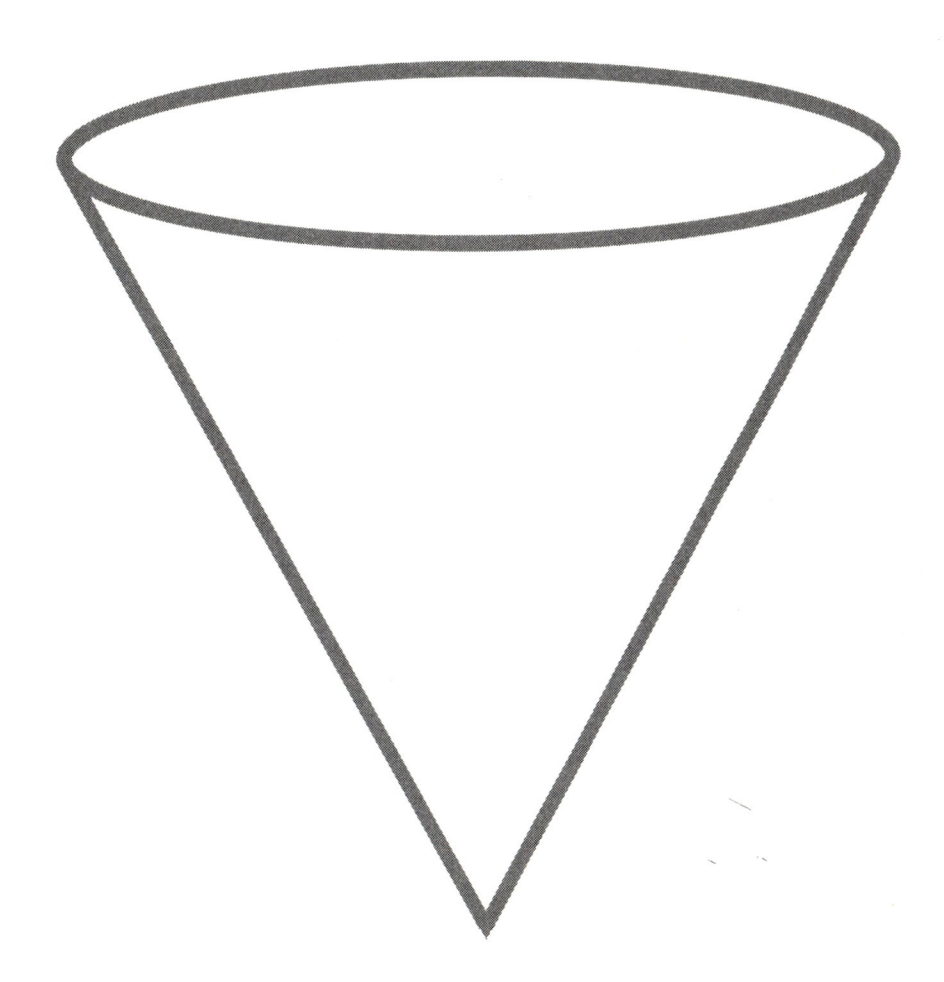

DO MORE

Draw a cone on your own with the vertex at the top of the drawing.

Modeling Name _____ Date _____

Draw a Sphere

Directions: Trace over the solid and dashed curves to draw the sphere. Keep as dashed curves when you trace.

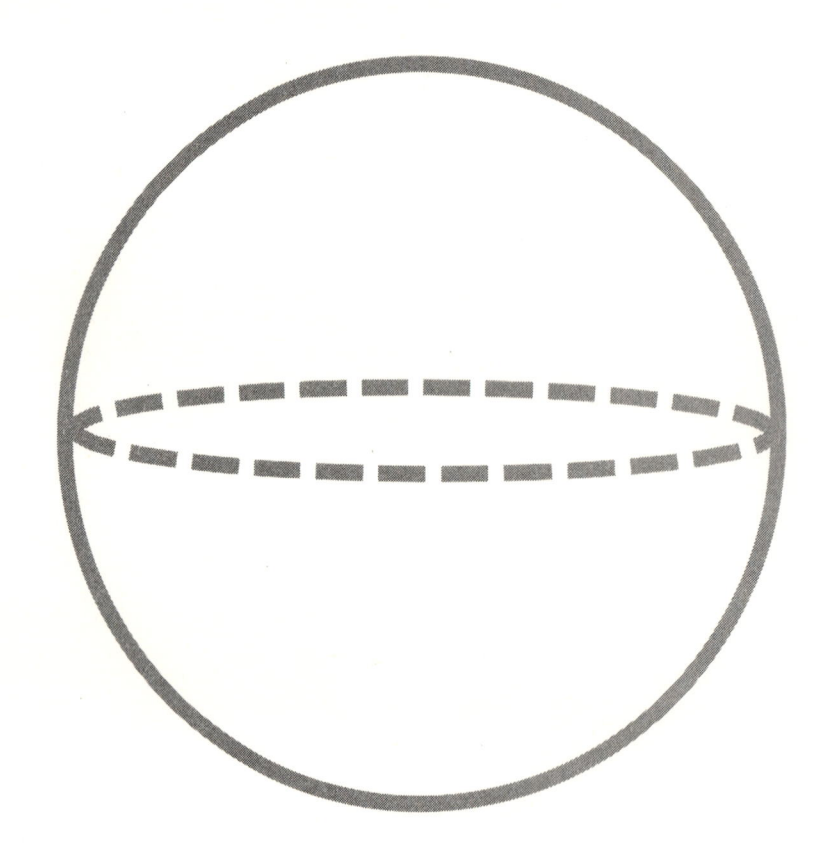

THINK

Describe how your drawing would look if you did not include the dashed oval.

Modeling

Name _____ Date _____

Net for a Cube

The **net** of a solid figure is a 2-dimensional drawing of the faces of a 3-dimensional solid figure. When the drawing is folded on its dotted lines, the solid figure is formed.

Directions: Cut out the net below. Fold on the dotted lines shown. Tape the edges to form a cube.

cube

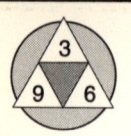

Net for a Square Pyramid

Directions: Cut out the net below. Fold on the dotted lines shown. Tape the edges to form a square pyramid.

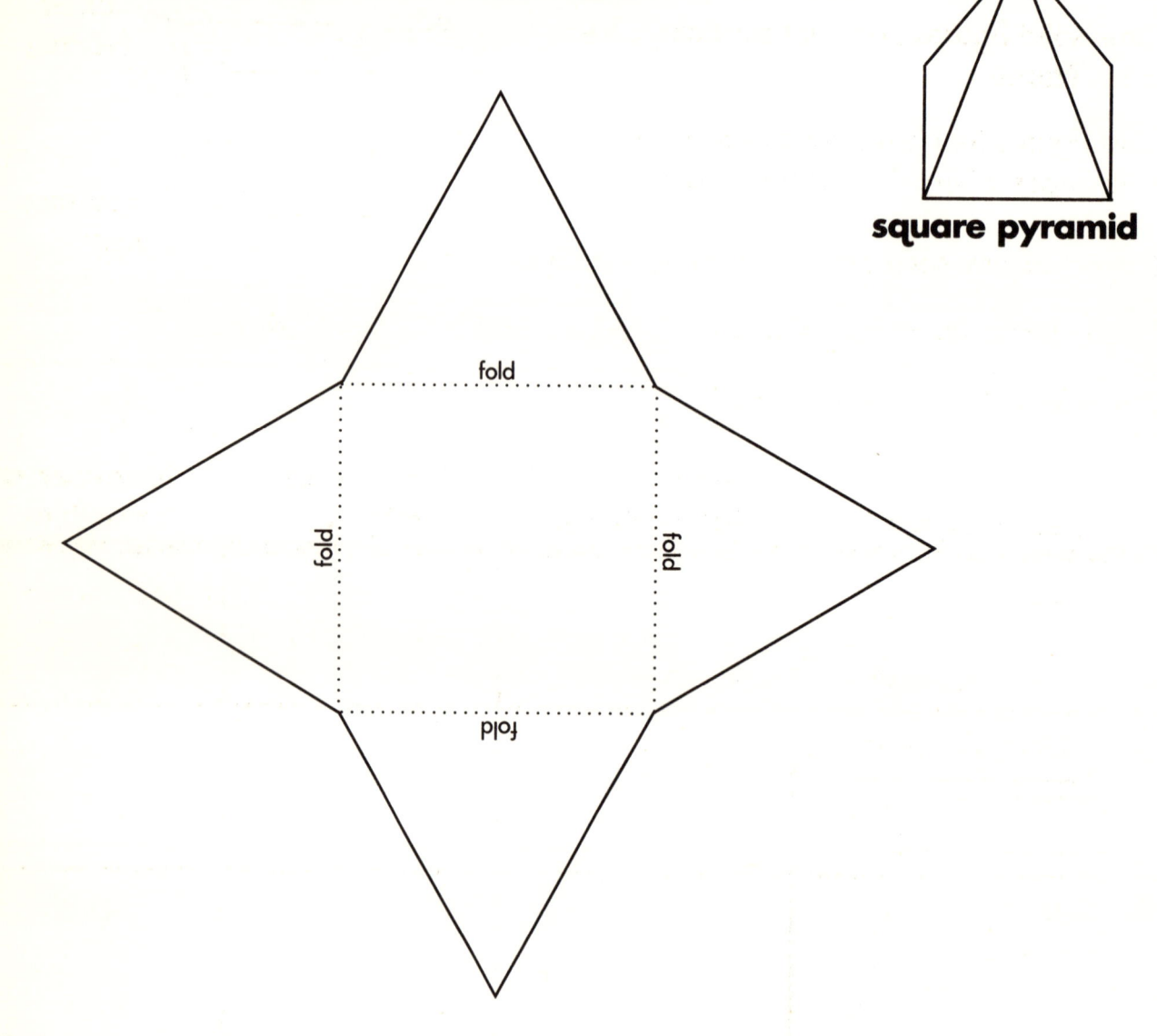

square pyramid

fold
fold
fold
fold

98

Flat Surfaces and Corners

Solid figures are 3-dimensional shapes.

Some solid figures have flat surfaces, often called **faces**.

Solid figures that have flat surfaces also have edges where the flat surfaces meet.

Corners of any solid figure are called **vertices**.

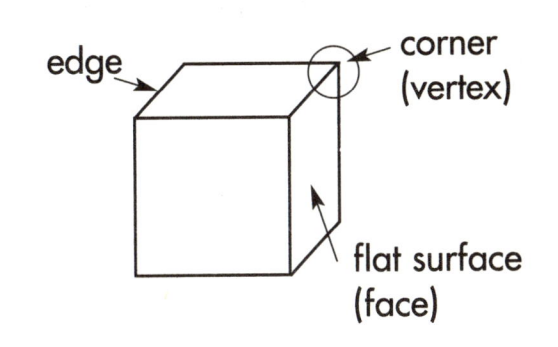

A cube has 6 flat surfaces (faces), 12 edges, and 8 corners (vertices).

Directions: Complete the table.

Solid Figure	Number of flat surfaces	Number of edges	Number of vertices
1. cube			
2. rectangular prism			
3. square pyramid			
4. triangular pyramid			

That's the Solid Figure

Directions: Circle the solid figure that is described.

1. A solid figure with 2 flat surfaces.

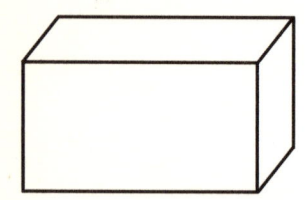

2. A solid figure that does not have any vertices.

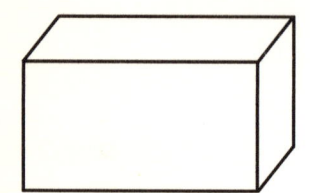

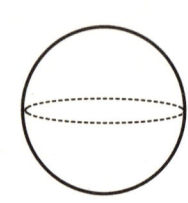

3. A solid figure whose net does not include a circle.

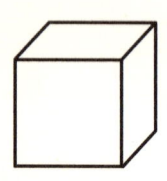

4. A solid figure with 6 flat surfaces and 12 edges.

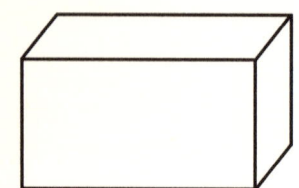

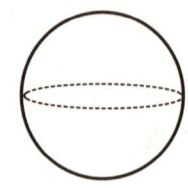

Modeling

Rectangular Prism Dot-to-Dot

Directions: Follow the steps and learn how to draw a rectangular prism.

5•   •8

1•   •4

6•   •7

2•   •3

Use solid line segments for Steps 1 – 3.

　　Step 1: Connect dots 1 to 2, 2 to 3, 3 to 4, and 4 to 1.

　　Step 2: Connect dots 5 to 8 and 8 to 7.

　　Step 3: Connect dots 1 to 5, 4 to 8, and 3 to 7.

Use dashed line segments for Step 4.

　　Step 4: Connect dots 5 to 6, 2 to 6, and 6 to 7.

THINK

Name the rectangle that you see as the front face of the prism by the numbers in the dot-to-dot.

Square Pyramid Dot-to-Dot

Directions: Follow the steps and learn how to draw a square pyramid.

•5

1•   •4

2•   •3

Use solid line segments for Steps 1 – 3.

    Step 1: Connect dots 1 to 2, 2 to 3, and 3 to 4.

    Step 2: Connect dots 5 to 1 and 5 to 4.

    Step 3: Connect dots 5 to 2 and 5 to 3.

Use dashed line segments for Step 4.

    Step 4: Connect dots 1 to 4.

Modeling

Name _____ Date _____

Looking from a Different View

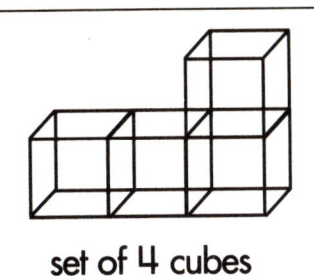

set of 4 cubes

Below are 2-dimensional views of the group of cubes at the left.

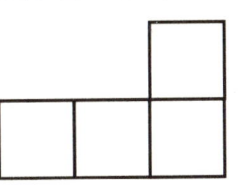

front and back views 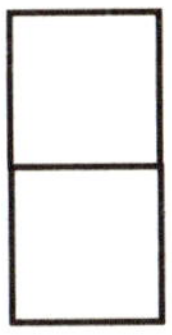   **side views**

Directions: Sketch the front and back views and side views of each set of cubes.

1.

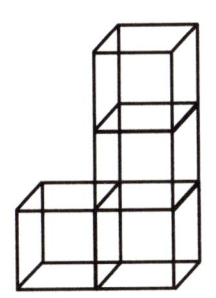

front and back views

side views

2.

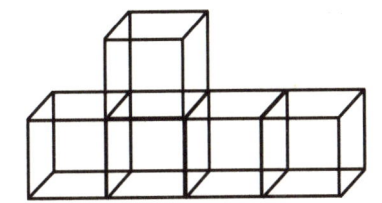

front and back views

side views

Building Stacks

Directions: Look at each of the views below. Use cubes to build each 3-dimensional object.

1.

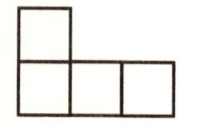

front and back views

side views

2.

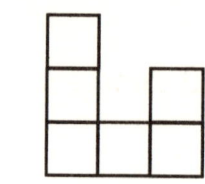

front and back views

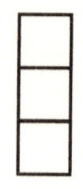

side views

3.

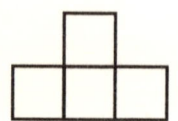

front and back views

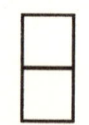

side views

4.

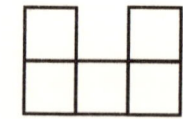

front and back views

side views

Modeling   Name _____   Date _____

Act as a Builder

Directions: Follow each instruction. Then sketch the front and back views and the side views of each set of cubes.

1. Use 6 cubes to build a 3-dimensional object.

   front and back views   side views

2. Use 10 cubes to build a 3-dimensional object.

   front and back views   side views

Modeling

Name _____ Date _____

Create Your Own Problems

1. Write a question about the perimeter of a polygon drawn on dot paper.

2. Write a word problem that involves using a cube.

3. Write instructions on how to draw a model of a cone.

4. Write a question about the number of flat surfaces, edges, and corners that a square pyramid has.

Modeling

Check Your Skills

1. Which solid figure is modeled by a cereal box?

   _____

2. Choose the figure that is the same size and same shape as the one at the right. Circle the figure.

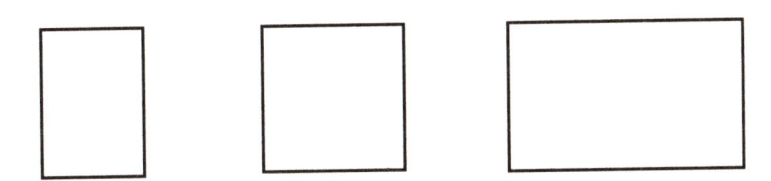

3. Name two solid figures that have no vertices.

   _____   _____

4. Draw a solid figure that can roll.

Check Your Skills (cont.)

5. What is the perimeter of a square with each side 2 centimeters long?

_____

6. What is the area of the square in question 5?

_____

7. How many squares make up the net for a cube?

_____

8. Which plane figure has two pairs of parallel sides and four right angles?

_____

9. Which solid figure has no flat surfaces, no edges, and no corners?

_____

Name _____ Date _____

Post Test

1. Draw a line that is parallel to the line below.

   ←——————————→

2. Draw a rectangle that is longer than it is tall.

3. Name a solid figure that has 0 edges and 2 flat surfaces.

   _____

4. Name the ordered pairs for each vertex of the triangle shown.

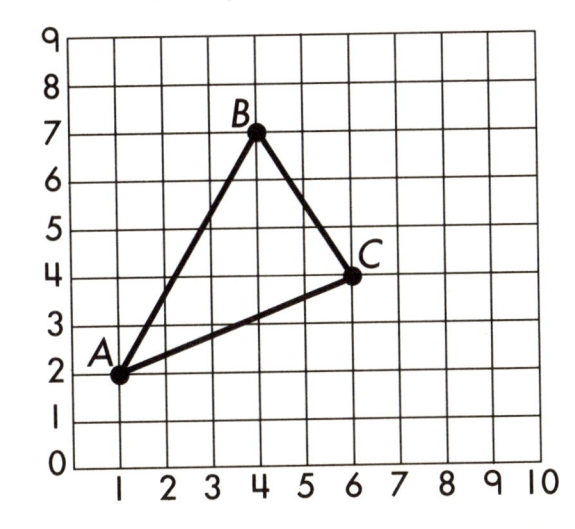

   A _____

   B _____

   C _____

109

Post Test (cont.)

5. How many lines of symmetry does a rectangle have?

_____

6. Circle the name of the transformation shown.

flip
slide
turn

7. On which side of T is M in the word TEAM?

_____

8. Draw a star above the moon?

9. Draw the dashed segments in the cube so that all faces of the cube can be seen.

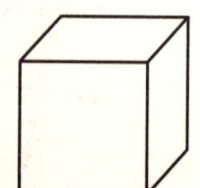

Answer Key

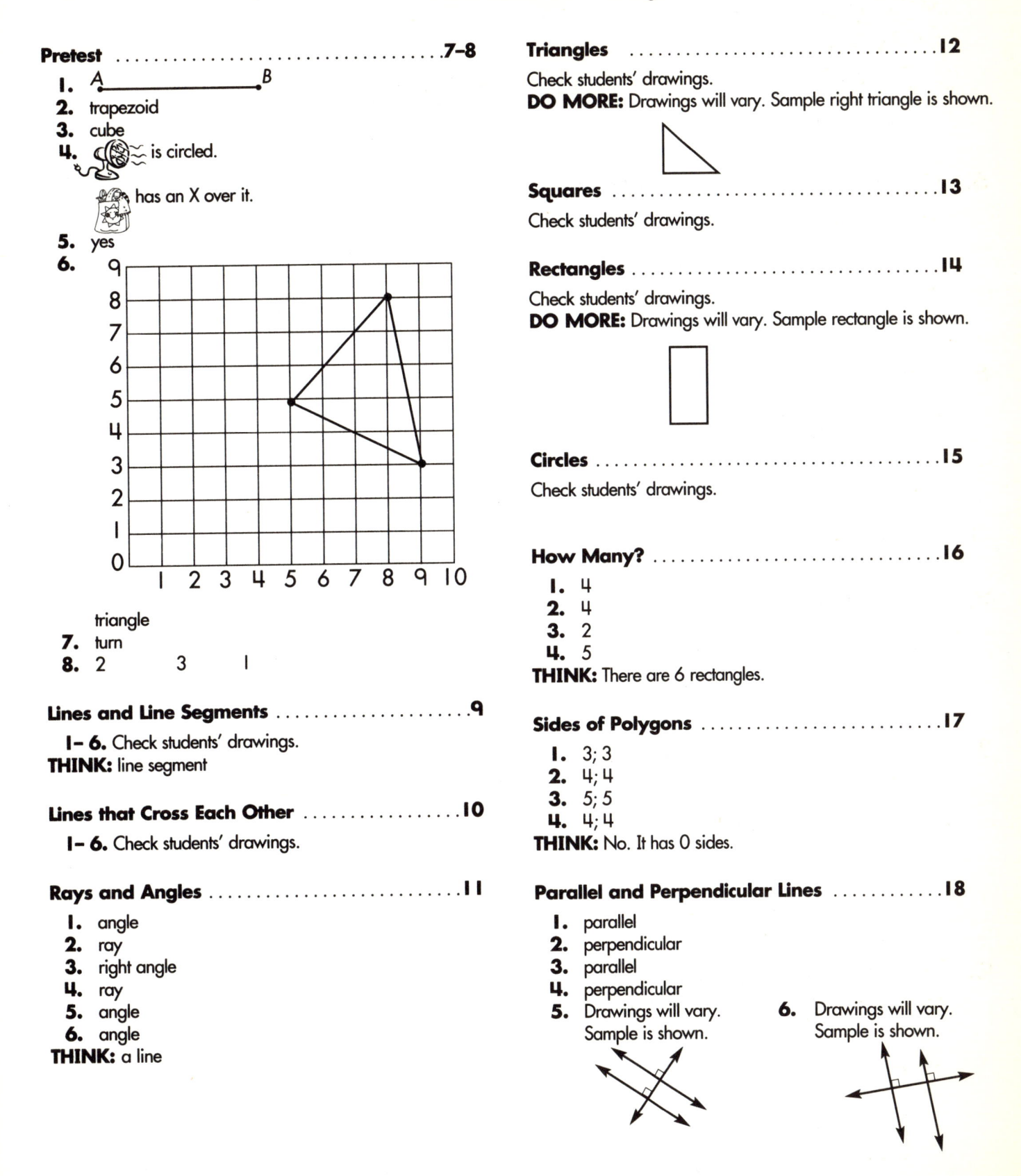

Pretest 7–8
1. A———B
2. trapezoid
3. cube
4. (fan) is circled.
   (bag) has an X over it.
5. yes
6. [graph showing triangle with vertices at (5,5), (8,8), (9,3)]
   triangle
7. turn
8. 2   3   1

Lines and Line Segments 9
1–6. Check students' drawings.
THINK: line segment

Lines that Cross Each Other 10
1–6. Check students' drawings.

Rays and Angles 11
1. angle
2. ray
3. right angle
4. ray
5. angle
6. angle
THINK: a line

Triangles 12
Check students' drawings.
DO MORE: Drawings will vary. Sample right triangle is shown.

Squares 13
Check students' drawings.

Rectangles 14
Check students' drawings.
DO MORE: Drawings will vary. Sample rectangle is shown.

Circles 15
Check students' drawings.

How Many? 16
1. 4
2. 4
3. 2
4. 5
THINK: There are 6 rectangles.

Sides of Polygons 17
1. 3; 3
2. 4; 4
3. 5; 5
4. 4; 4
THINK: No. It has 0 sides.

Parallel and Perpendicular Lines 18
1. parallel
2. perpendicular
3. parallel
4. perpendicular
5. Drawings will vary. Sample is shown.
6. Drawings will vary. Sample is shown.

Published by Instructional Fair. Copyright protected.

0-7424-2982-2 *Using the Standards: Geometry*

Answer Key

Quadrilaterals 19
1. irregular quadrilateral
2. not a quadrilateral
3. regular quadrilateral
4. irregular quadrilateral

THINK: Answers will vary. Sample answer: Speed Limit sign

Parallelograms 20
Check students' drawings.

Trapezoids 21
Check students' drawings.
DO MORE: Check students' drawings.

Pentagons 22
1. regular pentagon
2. irregular pentagon
3. Drawings will vary. Sample drawing is shown.

4. Drawings will vary. Sample drawing is shown.

Hexagons 23
Check students' drawings.

Octagons 24
Check students' drawings.
DO MORE: Drawings will vary. Most students will design a stop sign.

Regular and Irregular Figures 25

hexagon
octagon
pentagon
quadrilateral
triangle

Finish the Drawing 26
1 – 4. Check students' drawings.
THINK: Question 2 you can draw a square. Question 4 you can draw an equilateral triangle.

Joining Shapes 27
1 – 4. Check students' drawings.

Divide Into More 28
Drawings will vary. Sample drawings are shown.
1.
2.
3.
4.

DO MORE: Drawings will vary. Sample drawing is shown.

Answer Key

The Size of Shapes 29
1. X over fourth figure; third figure is colored.
2. X over fourth figure; second figure is colored.
3. X over third figure; fifth figure is colored.
4. X over third figure; first figure is colored.

Types of Triangles 30
1. equilateral
2. isosceles
3. scalene
4. isosceles

THINK: yes; no

Which Figure Am I? 31
1. first figure
2. first figure
3. first figure
4. first figure
5. third figure

DO MORE: Answers will vary.

Solid Figures 32
1. cylinder
2. cube
3. cone
4. rectangular prism

Objects that Model Solid Figures 33
1. sphere
2. cubes
3. cone
4. cube or rectangular prism
5. cylinder
6. cylinders

Faces, Edges, and Vertices 34
1. 6, 12
2. 8, 5
3. 1, 1
4. 12, 8

Plane Figure or Solid Figure 35
1. solid figure
2. solid figure
3. plane figure
4. solid figure

Which Solid Figure Am I? 36
1. cube (third figure)
2. cylinder (first figure)
3. cone (fourth figure)
4. rectangular prism (second figure)
5. sphere (first figure)

DO MORE: Answers will vary.

Stacking Solid Objects 37
1. bottom C, middle B, top A
2. bottom B, middle C, top A

Will It Roll? 38
1. never
2. sometimes
3. never
4. sometimes
5. never
6. always

DO MORE: Answers will vary. Sample answers: A ball always rolls. A can of soup sometimes rolls. A tissue box never rolls.

Create Your Own Problems 39
Answers will vary.

Check Your Skills 40-41
1. Drawings and explanations will vary. Samples are given.

   Opposite sides are parallel.
2. Drawings will vary. Samples are shown.

3. 5
4. cone
5. 6
6. no
7. regular
8. cube
9. Drawings will vary. Sample drawing is shown.

Published by Instructional Fair. Copyright protected.

0-7424-2982-2 Using the Standards: Geometry

Answer Key

The Toy Chest 42
1. left
2. right
3. right
4. right
5. left
6. left

Think: The N block is to the left of the R block.

Three Letter Words 43
1. too
2. joy
3. hat
4. say
5. arm
6. jet

DO MORE: Answers will vary. Sample answer: Write h on the left side of i. Write s on the right side of i.

Above and Below 44
Drawings will vary. Sample drawings are shown.
1. ○ / □
2. △ / V
3. ▭ / □
4. 🍎 / ⏢
5. M / ○
6. ▱ / T

Going Shopping 45
1. is left of
2. is under
3. is right of
4. is above
5. is left of
6. is above

Sunny or Cloudy 46
1. (sun above clouds)
2. (clouds above sun)
3. (clouds above sun)
4. (sun above clouds)

Study Time 47
1. (bed with books beside)
2. (table with books)

DO MORE: 10

Answer Key

In the Fish Bowl 48

1.
2.
3.
4.

THINK: 4

In Full Bloom 49-50

1-3.

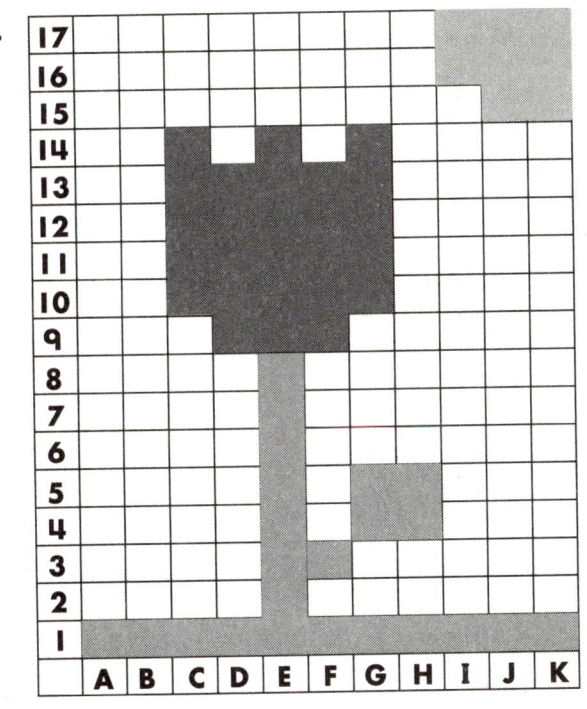

4. Answers will vary. Check students' drawings.

Directions to a Word 51

1. C
2. O
3. O
4. R
5. D
6. I
7. N
8. A
9. T
10. E

coordinate

About the Town 52
1. 10
2. 3
3. 2
4. Theater

THINK: Check students' answers.

Polygon People 53

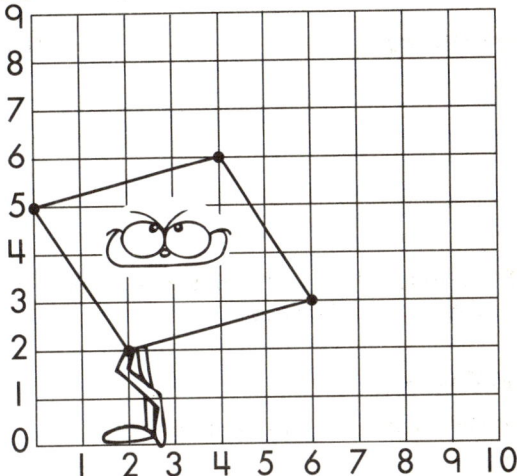

parallelogram
Check students' drawings.

End to End 54
1. A (2, 3); B (8, 7)
2. S (8, 8); T (8, 2)
3. G (7, 3); H (5, 7)
4. N (8, 4); P (2, 4)

THINK: Answers will vary but should include to read right 7 units and then up 3 units.

Length of Line Segments 55
1. 3 units
2. 5 units
3. 2 units
4. 5 units
5. 4 units
6. 6 units

THINK: Q is located at (0, 2).

Published by Instructional Fair. Copyright protected.

0-7424-2982-2 Using the Standards: Geometry

Answer Key

Plot for Distance 56

1–5.

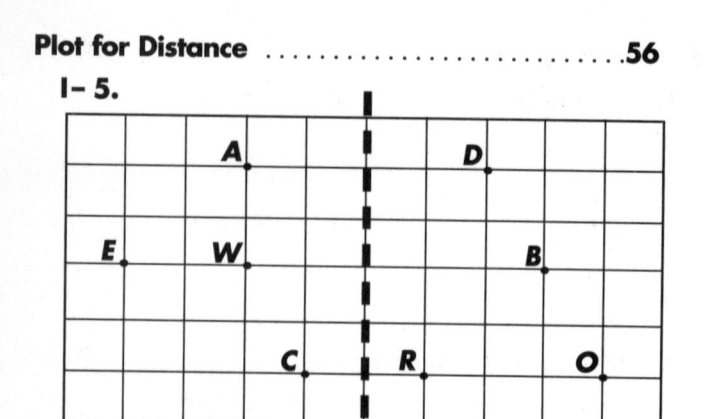

THINK: A and D; C and R

Lines of Symmetry 57

1. no
2. yes
3. yes
4. no
5. no
6. no

DO MORE: Check students' drawings.

Picture of Symmetry 58

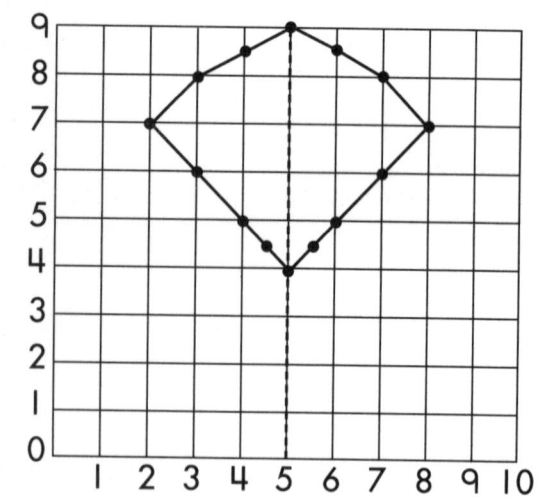

1–8. Students' ordered pairs will vary. Check students' answers.

Two Lines of Symmetry 59

Answers will vary for questions 2, 4, 5, and 6. Sample lines are shown.

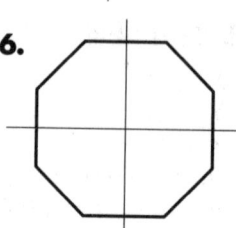

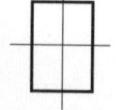

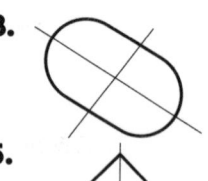

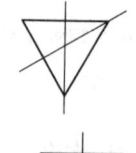

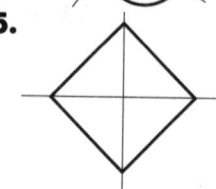

Draw with Symmetry 60

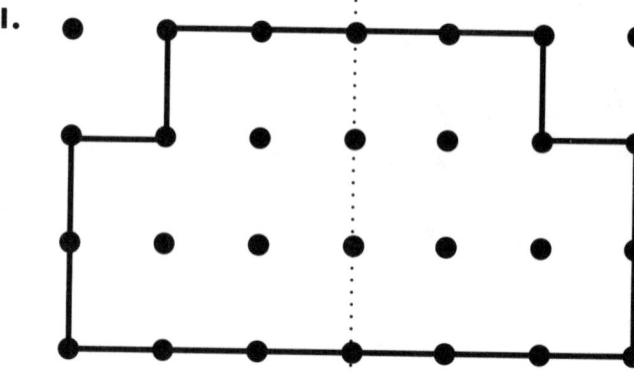

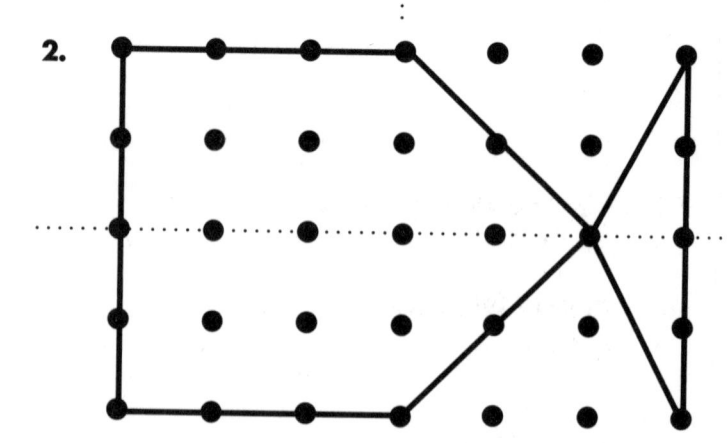

More Pictures with Symmetry 61

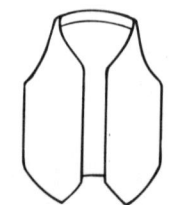

Published by Instructional Fair. Copyright protected.

0-7424-2982-2 Using the Standards: Geometry

Answer Key

Create Your Own Problems 62
Answers will vary.

Check Your Skills 63–64
1. X (8, 7)
   Y (6, 3)
   Z (3, 6)
2. The point should be graphed at (1, 2).
3. Answers will vary but should indicate that X is above and right of Y.
4. no
5. Drawings will vary. Sample drawing is shown.
6.

Flips 65
1. vertical
2. horizontal
3. horizontal
4. vertical

Slides 66
1. no
2. yes
3. no
4. yes

THINK: 2; If the left image is the original, the slide is right and down. 4. If the left image is the original, the slide is right and up.

Turns in Both Directions 67
1. clockwise
2. counterclockwise
3. clockwise
4. counterclockwise
5. clockwise

DO MORE:

Show a Flip, Slide, and Turn 68
Answers will vary. Sample answers are shown without color.
1.
2.
3.

Transformations 69
1.
2.
3.
4.
5.

Match the Transformation 70
1. first picture
2. second picture
3. second picture
4. second picture

DO MORE: Drawings will vary.

Transform Pattern Blocks 71–72
1. same
2.
3. same
4. same
5. same
6.

More Block Transformations 73–74
1. same
2.
3. same
4. same
5. same
6.

117

Published by Instructional Fair. Copyright protected.

0-7424-2982-2 Using the Standards: Geometry

Answer Key

Split in Half? 75
1. yes 2. yes
3. yes 4. no
5. no   6. no
THINK: 2 and 4

Symmetry in the World 76
1. no   2. yes
3. yes 4. no
THINK: The tassel is on the right side of the cap only.

Many Lines of Symmetry 77
1. 2   2. 1
3. 1   4. 0
5. 2   6. 4
7. 0

Point Symmetry 78
1. yes 2. yes
3. no   4. yes
5. no   6. yes

Create Your Own Problems 79
Answers will vary.

Check Your Skills 80-81
1. Answers will vary. Students could write 0, 1, or 8.
2. 1
3. horizontal flip
4.
5.
6. 8
7. no
8. a. m
   b. E

Shapes in Your World 82
Answers will vary.
THINK: Answers will vary.

Solid Figures in Your World 83
Answers will vary.
THINK: Answers will vary.

Use Dot Paper to Draw 84
1.
2.

THINK: Answers will vary. Sample answer: Dot paper helps you make line segments of equal length.

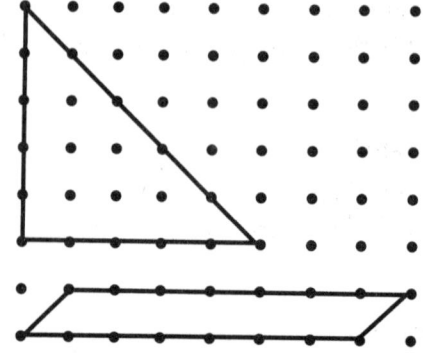

More Dot Paper Drawings 85
1—2.

THINK: isosceles triangle

Answer Key

Match Maker 86
1–3. Check students' drawings.

Congruent Shapes 87
1. congruent
2. not congruent
3. congruent

Perimeters on Dot Paper 88
A = 16
B = 18
C = 18
D = 18
Figure A

Areas on Dot Paper 89
The area of N is 12; Check students' drawings.
THINK: yes

Draw a Cube Using Dot Paper 90
Check students' drawings.
THINK: 6

Rectangular Prism on Dot Paper 91
Check students' drawings.
DO MORE: Check students' drawings.

Draw Another Cube 92
Check students' drawings.
THINK: The dashed segments shown on the inside of the cube.

Draw Another Prism 93
Check students' drawings.
THINK: Answers will vary but will most likely be another rectangle.

Draw a Cylinder 94
Check students' drawings.
THINK: The cylinder on the right makes the inside of cylinder visible.

Draw a Cone 95
Check students' drawings.
DO MORE: Check students' drawings.

Draw a Sphere 96
Check students' drawings.
THINK: It would look like a circle.

Net for a Cube 97
Check students' cube.

Net for a Square Pyramid 98
Check students' pyramid.

Flat Surfaces and Corners 99

	Number of flat surfaces	Number of edges	Number of vertices
1.	6	12	8
2.	6	12	8
3.	5	8	5
4.	4	6	4

That's the Solid Figure 100
1. cylinder (third figure)
2. sphere (third figure)
3. cube (first figure)
4. rectangular prism (first figure)

Rectangular Prism Dot-to-Dot 101

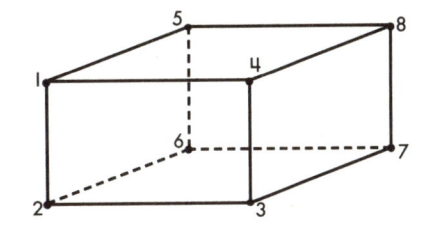

THINK: Answers will be either the rectangle 1–4 or rectangle 5–8.

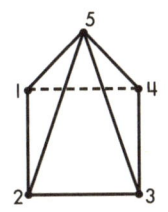

Square Pyramid Dot-to-Dot 102

Answer Key

Looking from a Different View 103

1. front and back views; side views
2. front and back views; side views

Building Stacks 104
Check students' arrangements.

Act as a Builder 105
Check students' drawings.

Create Your Own Problems 106
Answers will vary.

Check Your Skills 107-108
1. rectangular prism
2. first figure
3. sphere and cylinder
4. Drawings can be a sphere, cone, or cylinder.
5. 8 centimeters
6. 4 square centimeters
7. 6
8. square or rectangle
9. sphere

Post Test 109-110
1.
2.
3. cylinder
4. A (1, 2)
   B (4, 7)
   C (6, 4)
5. 2
6. turn
7. T is to the left of M
8.
9.

acute angle	edge
equilateral triangle	face
flip	intersecting lines

| a line segment where two faces of a solid figure meet | an angle that has a measure less than 90° |

| a flat surface of a solid figure | a triangle with 3 sides of equal length |

| lines that cross each other at one point | a transformation that creates a mirror image of the original image |

isosceles triangle	line of symmetry
net	ordered pair
parallel lines	parallelogram

a line that divides a picture or shape into two halves that are mirror images of each other	a triangle with 2 sides of equal length
a pair of numbers that describes the location of a point on a coordinate grid	a 2-dimensional drawing of the faces of a 3-dimensional solid figure
a quadrilateral with 2 pairs of parallel sides	lines that do not intersect each other

pentagon	perpendicular lines
quadrilateral	rectangle
right angle	scalene triangle

lines that intersect to form right angles	a five-sided plane figure
a parallelogram that has 4 right angles	a four-sided plane figure
a triangle that has no sides of equal length	an angle that forms a square corner (90°)

slide	square
triangle	trapezoid
turn	vertex

a rectangle that has 4 sides of equal length	a transformation that creates an image moved from the location of the original image
a quadrilateral with only one pair of parallel sides	a three-sided plane figure
a point where two line segments meet	a transformation that creates a rotated image of the original image